D0350592

To:

....

From:

....

Date:

....

The
Miracles
ANSWER BOOK

The
Miracles
ANSWER BOOK

LEE STROBEL
MARK MITTELBERG

ZONDERVAN

The Miracles Answer Book

© 2019 by Lee Strobel

This title is also available as a Zondervan ebook.

This title is also available as a Zondervan audio book.

Requests for information should be addressed to:
Zondervan, *3900 Sparks Dr. SE, Grand Rapids, Michigan 49546*

ISBN 978-0-310-33962-5

Art direction: Patti Evans

Interior design: Emily Ghattas

Printed in China

19 20 21 22 23   SKY   10 9 8 7 6 5 4 3 2 1

Contents

Introduction

It took the compelling historical evidence for a miracle—the resurrection—to convince an atheist like me that Jesus really is the unique Son of God. But my skeptical nature didn't disappear when I became a Christian. I wanted to know: *Is God still in the miracle business today?*

This launched me on a two-year investigation into the supernatural, a journey that took me to unexpected places and provocative conclusions. What I learned left me flabbergasted as I probed eye-popping cases in which God unmistakably intervened in people's lives in dramatic and well-documented ways. You'll read about some of them in the coming pages, so get ready to be amazed!

Yet I also encountered instances in which charlatans falsely claimed miracles had occurred or where people exaggerated circumstances to make it look like a miracle happened when it clearly didn't. If there's one lesson I learned in this process, it's that care and discernment are needed whenever we investigate the miraculous.

In fact, this word of caution is important: "Do not quench the Spirit. Do not treat prophecies with contempt but test them all; hold on to what is good, reject every kind of evil" (1 Thessalonians 5:19–22). An appropriate application of that verse for us might be, "Do not treat *miracle claims* with contempt but test them all; hold on to what is good."

In other words, don't reject unusual stories out of hand, but don't uncritically accept them either. Be neither cynical nor gullible. Instead, scrutinize claims of the miraculous with the goal of discovering what might be genuine works from a supernatural source. The same Source who promised, "You will seek me and find me when you seek me with all your heart" (Jeremiah 29:13).

It's with that goal in mind that I wrote my larger volume, *The Case for Miracles*.[1] Now my ministry associate Mark Mittelberg and I have produced this question-and-answer book to cover the key issues involving God's supernatural intervention in our world. I believe you'll find it to be helpful and inspiring at the same time.

Let me urge you to approach these topics with an open heart and mind. Ask the "God of Wonders" to lead you into all truth and to bless you as you seek and follow him. You'll emerge with a deeper faith and a more profound sense of awe in God's majesty, creativity, and love for each of us.

Lee Strobel

1

What do you mean by
miracle? I hear that term
used in so many ways.

So do I—sometimes even by myself! I was recently driving through downtown Houston, its streets choked with cars at rush hour, as I inched toward a skyscraper where I was due for a meeting. Suddenly, against all odds, I spotted a vacant parking space adjacent to the door.

"A miracle," I mused—and maybe it was. Or maybe it wasn't. The truth is that we often throw around that term too loosely.

Not long ago I set my computer to search for the keyword *miracle* among the news stories on the Internet, and all sorts of articles popped up:

- "Boat captain rescues 'miracle' cat thrown off bridge"

- "Miracle on Water Street: A doctor witnesses crash, saves man's life"
- "Miracle baby born the size of a tennis ball now home"
- A football player was said to need a "miracle" to resuscitate his sagging career
- A diver who survived hitting his head on the platform is called a "miracle man"

So what's the best way to define the miraculous? Philosophers and theologians have offered various descriptions. Augustine was poetic, saying a miracle is "whatever appears that is difficult or unusual above the hope and power of them who wonder." Scottish philosopher David Hume was skeptical: "A miracle is a violation of the laws of nature." Oxford's Richard Swinburne was straightforward, calling a miracle "an event of an extraordinary kind, brought about by a god, and of religious significance."[1]

Personally, I'm partial to the definition offered by the late Richard L. Purtill, professor emeritus of philosophy at Western Washington University:

A miracle is an event:

1. brought about by the power of God that is
2. a temporary
3. exception
4. to the ordinary course of nature
5. for the purpose of showing that God has acted in history.[2]

This obviously sets real miracles apart from much of what is described today as "miraculous"—including, I'll have to admit, my finding a parking spot in Houston's rush hour!

2

Can you explain the difference between a divine miracle and an ordinary coincidence?

Richard L. Purtill, whose definition of miracles I quoted in the previous answer, recounted how he was once prescribed nitroglycerine tablets for a heart condition. The pharmacist said something that stuck in his mind: if two pills taken in succession don't relieve the pain, take a third but immediately call an ambulance.

Not long afterward, he awoke with chest pain. He took one pill and later another, but neither had an effect. He took a third, and his wife called 911. The paramedics arrived promptly, and his life was saved.

After he recovered, he had a flat tire on a car trip and his heart stopped while he was changing the tire. He fell unconscious, his head on the freeway. Two passing motorists stopped; both of them just happened to know CPR. One called the paramedics. Purtill's heart was restarted, and his life was spared once more.

Although he said he's grateful to God for the outcome, Purtill stressed that "there was nothing in the events to suggest any non-natural causes. The pharmacist's remarks, the training of the people who helped me, the medical technology are all things that seem to need no non-natural explanation."

Consequently, he doesn't consider his survival to be miraculous. On the other hand, he does believe as a Christian that "God was, as usual, hiding divine action in plain sight amid the ordinary course of events."[1]

So some of what we casually classify as "miracles" really seem closer to fortunate coincidences. How can we tell them apart? When I see something extraordinary that has spiritual overtones and is validated by an independent source or event, that's when the "miracle" bell goes off in my mind.

In other words, a dream about a nebulous figure writing chemistry problems on a blackboard wouldn't be miraculous in itself. But if those equations then correspond to the very same problems that present themselves on an examination the next day, that seems miraculous—especially if the event occurs after a prayer pleading for God's help.

Spontaneous remissions sometimes happen in serious illnesses, but they usually take place over a period of time and often are transient. But if a serious illness is instantly and permanently eradicated at the exact moment a prayer for healing is being offered—well, that would probably push the needle over into the "miracle" category for me.

So, when trying to determine whether something is a miracle, the circumstances surrounding the event often matter as much as the event itself.

3

Aren't a lot of miracle claims just plain weird—like people who see Jesus' face on their burned burrito?

Absolutely. And as much as I like burritos, I have to wonder whether Jesus would manifest a miracle with something so obviously fattening!

But it gets weirder than that. Just scan the Internet for "strange miracles" and you'll read stories about birds that consulted with saints, religious people levitating above the clouds, statues and paintings that weep, and, of course, Jesus' face showing up not only on burritos, but also on pieces of toast, potato chips, tortillas, pizzas and pancakes, sliced oranges, inside the caps of Marmite jars, on Walmart receipts, garage doors, in the clouds, and even on the moldy trim next to an old bathtub.

Is it possible some of those are actual signs

from God? I guess that's possible, but to most observers these things come across as fake news or speculative rumors. Generally, these are easily discarded or at best become interesting curiosities. But they have no bearing on our lives—and they certainly don't tell us anything about the validity of serious miracle claims.

Worse, these kinds of examples can sometimes be used by deceitful people to draw the gullible into their religious group or sect. Peter distanced himself from such things when he said, "We did not follow cleverly devised stories when we told you about the coming of our Lord Jesus Christ in power, but we were eyewitnesses of his majesty" (2 Peter 1:16). He also warned about false prophets who, "in their greed . . . will exploit you with fabricated stories" (2 Peter 2:3).

Paul was even more pointed:

> Do not let anyone who delights in false humility and the worship of angels disqualify you. Such a person also goes into great detail about what they have seen; they are puffed up with

idle notions by their unspiritual mind. They have lost connection with the head, from whom the whole body, supported and held together by its ligaments and sinews, grows as God causes it to grow. (Colossians 2:18–19)

Also, if you look back at the definition of biblical miracles that I presented in the first chapter, these strange examples almost always miss the mark.

So, my advice would be to ignore these odd and meaningless claims. Focus instead on finding the truth about the genuine works of the Creator, with the goal of knowing him and his supernatural blessings in your life.

4

How common are miracles? Aren't they pretty rare?

That's what I used to think—but then I started my investigation into the miraculous. As I began researching this topic, my curiosity prompted me to commission a national scientific survey, which was conducted by Barna Research.[1]

What did we discover? Interestingly, half of US adults (51 percent) said they believe that the miracles of the Bible happened as they are described. The numbers, however, were lower among millennials (ages eighteen to thirty) compared to baby boomers (ages fifty to sixty-eight) by 43 percent versus 55 percent.

Asked whether miracles are possible today, two out of three Americans (67 percent) said yes, with only 15 percent saying no. The others weren't sure. Again, there were generational differences, with young adults less likely (61 percent) to believe than boomers (73 percent). Incidentally, Republicans were more likely to believe in modern miracles (74 percent) than Democrats (61 percent)—a statistic on which I offer no comment.

I was interested in what was generating the skepticism of those who don't think miracles can occur these days. The biggest reasons turned out to be a lack of belief in the supernatural (44 percent) and the contention that modern science has ruled out the possibility of miracles (20 percent). While only 12 percent of those age sixty-nine and older cited science as their obstacle, that number doubled among millennials.

Most of all, I wanted to know how many people have had an experience that they can explain only as being a miracle of God. I found that a surprising number of Americans believe God has intervened supernaturally in their lives.

As it turns out, *nearly two out of five US adults (38 percent) said they have had such an experience*— which by extrapolation means that an eye-popping *94,792,000* Americans are convinced that God has performed at least one miracle for them personally.[2]

Even weeding out instances that were actually just coincidences, as many of those undoubtedly would be, that still leaves a surprising number of seemingly supernatural events. Among various age groups, the data stayed fairly consistent: 35.5 percent among millennials and 39.7 percent among boomers.

The conclusion? It seems that miracles are not nearly as rare as we might assume.

5

Aren't claims of miracles more common among uneducated people?

That is only partially true. Going back to the study I commissioned on the topic, we found that the percentage of people who claimed to have personally experienced a miracle decreased with education—41 percent of those with a high school diploma said they have had a divine intervention, compared to 29 percent of college graduates. The same was true for income levels, with more skepticism among the wealthy.

But before jumping to conclusions, we should step back and ask which part is the effect and which is the cause. Do certain groups fail to recognize miracles because they consider themselves "too smart" for such things? Maybe they aren't open and thus preclude themselves from even considering that some of their own experiences might have been miraculous. Let's face it: people who don't believe in buried treasures are rarely the ones who find them!

There's also an interesting verse in the Bible that says, "You do not have because you do not ask God" (James 4:2). Might more people experience miracles if they actually asked God for them? Also, we're told in Matthew 13:58 that when Jesus was in his hometown of Nazareth, "he did not do many miracles there because of their lack of faith."

Could it be that the more educated and wealthy don't experience as many miracles as others simply because they don't ask for or expect them? The current culture of skepticism in our schools and universities certainly serves to diminish the faith of their students—thus, it would seem, diminishing their openness to the miraculous.

And get this: although skeptic Harriet Hall dismissed supernatural reports as being "more common from the uncivilized and uneducated,"[1] a 2004 survey showed that 55 percent of US physicians have seen results in their patients that they

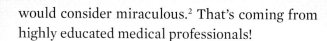

would consider miraculous.[2] That's coming from highly educated medical professionals!

In fact, a full three-quarters of the 1,100 doctors surveyed are convinced that miracles can occur today—a percentage that's actually higher than the US population in general.[3]

I'd say the rumor that miracles are only for the simple among us is simply not true.

6

Have you heard stories of
dreams that you would
consider to be miraculous?

In an earlier entry, I referenced a situation
where answers to a chemistry exam were given
in a dream the night before the test. That really
is a dream scenario for a student facing a crucial
exam, isn't it? I sure could have used some dreams
like that when I was working on my degree at Yale
Law School! Unfortunately, that never happened
to me, but here's something that actually *did*
happen—interestingly, to another student at Yale.

Benjamin, who had scored the highest SAT
ranking of any student in twenty years from a
Detroit public school, entered Yale with a full
scholarship. He viewed himself as something
special—until the end of his first semester.

Ben was failing chemistry, a prerequisite

16

to fulfilling his dream of becoming a physician. Everything depended on the final exam. But he wasn't even close to being ready for it.

That evening, he prayed. "Lord, medicine is the only thing I ever wanted to do," he said. "Would you please tell me what it is *you* really want me to do?"

He intended to study for the exam all night, but he soon fell asleep. All seemed lost—until he had a dream: he was alone in an auditorium when a nebulous figure began writing chemistry problems on the blackboard.

"When I went to take the test the next morning, it was like *The Twilight Zone*," he recalled. "I recognized the first problem as one of the ones I had dreamed about. And the next, and the next, and the next—and I aced the exam and got a good mark in chemistry. And I promised the Lord he would never have to do that for me again."

Ben went on to achieve his goal of becoming a physician. By age thirty-three, he became the youngest director of pediatric neurosurgery in the country, performing pioneering operations at

Johns Hopkins Hospital. He separated twins conjoined at the brain, performed the first successful neurosurgery on a fetus, developed new methods of treating brain-stem and spinal-cord tumors, and was awarded the nation's highest civilian honor, the Presidential Medal of Freedom.

What's more, a 2014 poll ranked Benjamin Solomon Carson Sr. as among the ten most admired people in America. But he probably never would have gotten there if he hadn't asked God for assistance—and been given a dream that helped him pass a chemistry course nearly fifty years ago.[1]

So yes, that's one example of many that I can give of dreams I consider to be from a supernatural source.

7

You were once a skeptical journalist. What made you start believing in miracles?

That's true—and a good question! A former colleague from the *Chicago Tribune* recently expressed surprise that I had turned from atheism to following Christ. He said, "You were one of the most skeptical people I knew. If I told you the deli down the block had a good sandwich, you wouldn't believe me until I produced a dozen restaurant reviews plus a certified chemical analysis of the ingredients from the Food and Drug Administration."

While that was overstated (*a bit*), my background in journalism and law did tend to amplify my naturally doubting personality. The newsroom, with its prevailing attitude of scoffing skepticism, was an ideal environment for me. And yet, ironically, it was my skepticism that ultimately drove me to faith in Jesus.

As you may have read in *The Case for Christ* or seen in the movie by the same name, it was my wife Leslie's newfound belief in Christ that provoked me to investigate the historical underpinnings of Christianity. I was confident that my objections would end up undermining the entire religion and rescuing her from this Jesus "cult."

To my dismay, the data of science (from cosmology and physics to biochemistry and human consciousness) convinced me there was a supernatural Creator, while the evidence from history satisfied me that Jesus of Nazareth was resurrected from the dead, confirming his identity as the unique Son of God.

The inexorable conclusion that Christianity is true prompted me to put my trust in Christ and later leave my newspaper career to spend my life telling others the story of his atoning death on their behalf.

However, my skeptical nature didn't disappear. Did I believe in miracles? Yes, of course, I was convinced that the resurrection and other miracles occurred as the Gospels reported. But that left open the question of whether God is still supernaturally intervening in people's lives in the twenty-first century.

I agreed with pastor and author Timothy Keller, who said, "There is nothing illogical about miracles if a Creator God exists. If a God exists who is big enough to create the universe in all its complexity and vastness, why should a mere miracle be such a mental stretch?"[1]

But that wasn't enough. I had to check it out for myself—and when I did, I became completely convinced that God is still in the miracle business today.

8

Have you ever seen an
actual miracle?

If you saw *The Case for Christ* movie, you got a
glimpse of the amazing ways God worked in
both Leslie's life and mine. I believe that each time
someone trusts in Christ, God performs a spiritual
miracle in him or her. That was certainly the case
for us.

The tension you feel between the characters
playing Leslie and me in the movie was not some
dramatic element invented by the screenwriter. It
was all too real. In fact, when Leslie told me she
had decided to follow Jesus, the first word to enter
my mind was *divorce*. I was sure I didn't want to be
married to some Jesus freak!

Then as I began doing my research, God
started to do something supernatural. As the
movie portrays, Leslie was praying the promise

daily from Ezekiel 36:26: "I will give you a new heart and put a new spirit within you; and I will remove the heart of stone . . . and give you a heart of flesh" (NASB).

God answered that prayer, and while the evidence was changing my mind, God's Spirit was changing my heart. Frankly, I think *that* took a miracle!

In addition, Leslie and I have seen God's mysterious work in our own lives as followers of Christ. For example, one day during prayer I felt prompted to send an anonymous five-hundred-dollar cashier's check to a young lady in our church who was struggling to recover from a life of abuse and financial difficulty.

Leslie prayed and felt the same urging. We knew this wasn't something conjured from our own minds because that amount constituted almost everything we had in the bank at the time. Moreover, we felt compelled to mail the check so it would arrive the following Monday.

On Monday morning, before that woman's mail had arrived, she called me in a panic. "Please pray for me," she pleaded. "My car broke down Saturday afternoon, and they said it will cost almost five hundred dollars to fix. I just don't have the money! I don't know what to do!"

"Okay," I said, trying to conceal my excitement. "Leslie and I will pray for you."

That afternoon she received the anonymous check, and Leslie and I experienced the joy of being the answer to the sincere prayers of a sister in Christ.

Coincidence? To me, it was an extraordinary example of an ongoing pattern of God's supernatural activity in our lives.

9

Have you ever seen or
experienced a divine healing?

Immediately after our daughter Alison was
born, she struggled with a mysterious, life-
threatening illness. Some Christian friends prayed
earnestly for her (I was still an atheist), and then
suddenly and inexplicably she was healthy again.
The doctors never understood what had happened,
but it seems clear to me today that our healthy
daughter is a testament to God's intervention.

Also, early in my Christian life I too went
through a serious and unexplained episode with my
own health, and this time Leslie and I prayed for
healing. A few days later I returned to full health.
Neither we nor my doctors ever understood what
happened, but Leslie and I believe God answered
our sincere prayers.

One of the most clear-cut miracles I've ever

"experienced," though, is one you can experience in the same way—by listening to the recording of a healing as it happened. I'm talking about the story of Duane Miller, a pastor whose greatest enjoyment came from preaching and singing at his small church in Texas.[1]

When he awoke with the flu one morning, his throat was like sandpaper and his voice would "catch" on words. Each syllable was painful. The flu soon disappeared, but his windpipe remained ablaze and his voice was reduced to a raspy whisper.

For all practical purposes, Miller's voice was gone. No longer able to preach, he resigned from his pastorate. Over the next three years he was examined by sixty-three physicians. The diagnosis: the flu virus had destroyed the nerves of his vocal cords, rendering them limp. When he asked about his prognosis for recovery, a doctor told him, "Zero."

Later, despite Miller's protestations, his former Sunday school class prevailed on him to speak. A special microphone was used to amplify Miller's hoarse, croaky voice.

The text he spoke on, interestingly, was Psalm 103, which talks about God's ability to heal. As he taught, his choking sensation suddenly disappeared. "For the first time in three years, I could breathe freely," he recalled. "I heard a gasp from the crowd, and that's when I, too, realized my voice had come back."

His stunned audience began to clap and cheer; his wife, Joylene, broke down in tears. Subsequent doctor examinations showed his throat looked as if it never had any problems; in fact, even the scar tissue had disappeared. Today, Miller is a pastor once again and, ironically, he speaks daily on his own radio program.

Does God heal today? I'm convinced that in many cases he does.

10

Why do you think miracles are so important?

Miracles are obviously important to the person on the receiving end of God's supernatural healing or provision. I don't think anyone who has experienced one would argue with that!

But miracles are important in a much broader way; they matter because they grab people's attention and, in many cases, they serve to change people's minds about God and his offer of forgiveness and leadership in their lives.

Jesus once said to a crowd of resistant listeners, "Do not believe me unless I do the works of my Father. But if I do them, even though you do not believe me, believe the works, that you may know and understand that the Father is in me, and I in the Father" (John 10:37–38). In other words, he was telling them to let the miraculous works he had performed persuade them of the validity of his message.

We can see this linkage played out in Mark 2, where Jesus was teaching in Capernaum, and some men brought their paralyzed friend to him in the hope that Jesus would heal him. After discovering how crowded the house was where Jesus was teaching, they cut a hole in the roof and lowered their friend through the opening. Seeing their faith, Jesus said to the paralyzed man, "Son, your sins are forgiven" (v. 5).

This surprised and concerned the religious leaders who were present because they knew only God could forgive sins. So they—not understanding who Jesus really was—considered his statement to be blasphemy.

Here's what Mark 2:8–12 tells us happened next:

> Immediately Jesus knew in his spirit that this was what they were thinking in their hearts, and he said to them, "Why are you thinking these things? Which is easier: to say to this

paralyzed man, 'Your sins are forgiven,' or to say, 'Get up, take your mat and walk'? But I want you to know that the Son of Man has authority on earth to forgive sins." So he said to the man, "I tell you, get up, take your mat and go home." He got up, took his mat and walked out in full view of them all.

Jesus explicitly explained the purpose of his miracle here—he said he was going to heal the man so they would "know that the Son of Man has authority on earth to forgive sins." Then, after the man stood up, grabbed his mat, and walked out in front of everyone, verse 12 tells us, "This amazed everyone and they praised God, saying, 'We have never seen anything like this!'"

This was a clear illustration of how important miracles can be, leading people to trust and worship the God behind the miraculous.

11

Can miracles really persuade
skeptics today?

Let me tell you about Dr. Craig Keener, a
scholar I interviewed for my book *The Case
for Miracles.* As a young man Keener was an atheist, but he remembers once saying, "If somebody
is out there—if there's a God or gods—then please
show me."

Soon after that he was walking home from
school when a couple of Christians challenged
him. Their evangelistic approach was really rough,
and they didn't have the knowledge they needed
to answer Keener's questions, but God used the
encounter just the same.

"As I walked home," he told me, "I felt con-
victed by the Holy Spirit. I passed a Catholic church
and saw a cross atop the steeple. I knew about
the Trinity, and I wondered whether the Trinity

was looking down on me. I finally got to my bedroom, where I began arguing back and forth with myself—*This can't be right. But what if it is?* And then I sensed it."

"Sensed what?" I asked.

"God's very presence—right there, right then, right in my room. I had been wanting empirical evidence, but instead God gave me something else: the evidence of his presence. I was simply overwhelmed by the palpable presence of God. It was like Someone was right there in the room with me, and it wasn't something I was generating because it wasn't what I was necessarily wanting."

"How did you respond?" I asked.

"I said, 'God, those guys said Jesus died for me and rose again and that's what saves me. If that's what you're saying, I'll accept it. But I don't understand how that works. So if you want to save me, you're going to have to do it yourself.'"

"And did he?"

"All of a sudden, I felt something rushing through my body that I'd never experienced before. I jumped up and said, 'What was that?' I knew God had come into my life. At that moment I was filled with wonder and worship."

Two days later, Keener walked to a nearby church, where the pastor asked him, "Are you sure you've been saved?" Keener said, "No, I don't know if I did it right." So the minister led him in a prayer of repentance and faith.

"I felt the same overwhelming sense of God's majesty and greatness and awesomeness," Keener told me. "I felt a kind of joy I'd never experienced before. And for the first time, I understood what my purpose was. What *the* purpose is . . . to live for him, to serve him, to worship him."

That's one of many examples, but yes—the miraculous often convinces skeptics even today.

12

David Hume said miracles would violate the laws of nature, and therefore they are impossible. Your response?

David Hume was one of history's most famous skeptics. Although he lived in the eighteenth century, one atheist told me Hume's case against miracles is still "a knock-down argument" today.

But is Hume's reputation warranted? I posed that question to Dr. Craig Keener. "Well, let's be honest: his arguments against miracles are based on presuppositions and circular reasoning," he told me.

"Give me an example," I said.

"Hume defines 'miracle' as a violation of natural law, and he defines 'natural law' as being principles that cannot be violated. So he's ruling out the possibility of miracles at the outset. He's assuming that which he's purporting to prove, which is circular reasoning. In fact, it's an anti-supernatural bias, not a cogent philosophical argument."

"Is he wrong to call miracles a violation of the laws of nature?" I asked.

"Today we understand laws as *describing* the normal pattern of nature, not *prescribing* them. In other words . . ." He turned in his chair to retrieve a ballpoint pen from his desk, holding it up for me to see. "If I drop this pen, the law of gravity tells me it will fall to the floor. But if I were to reach in and grab the pen in midair, I wouldn't be violating the law of gravity; I would merely be intervening. And certainly if God exists, he would have the ability to intervene in the world that he himself created."

Then Keener added. "Hume simply rejects any evidence that contradicts his thesis."

I asked, "What about Hume's claim that the uniform experience of humankind is that miracles don't happen?"

"That's an assertion, not an argument. What he's saying is, 'Miracles violate the principle that miracles never happen.'[1] Again, notice how circular that is. In addition, his criteria for evaluating miracles are too vague and even contradictory. For instance, he would require any witnesses to be of unquestioned good sense, but then he appears to question the good sense of anyone who claims to have witnessed a miracle."

Other scholars concur with Keener's criticisms. David Johnson, who earned his doctorate in philosophy at Princeton University, said Hume's arguments on miracles are "entirely without merit."[2] He added, "The view that there is in Hume's essay . . . any argument or reply or objection that is even superficially good, much less powerful or devastating, is simply a philosophical myth."[3]

13

How can we best scrutinize stories about miracles?

That's a question I have wrestled with myself. When I had the chance to interview Dr. Craig Keener, I asked him how he thought people should look at claims of miracles.

"I think we should look at the evidence with a healthy dose of skepticism but also with an open mind," he began. "Are there eyewitnesses? When we have multiple, independent, and reliable witnesses, this increases the probability that their testimony is accurate. Do the witnesses have a reputation for honesty? Do they have something to gain or lose? Did they have a good opportunity to observe what occurred? Is there corroboration? Are there any medical records? What were the precise circumstances and timing of the event?

Are there alternative naturalistic explanations for what happened?"

I pointed out that atheist professor Jerry Coyne said that "massive, well-documented and either replicated or independently corroborated evidence from multiple and reliable sources" would be needed to have confidence in a miracle.[1]

"Replicable?" Keener replied. "Miracles are one-offs. They are part of history, which can't be repeated. How could we test whether a person was brought back from the dead—shoot him and try again? I don't think so," he said, chuckling. "But aside from that, we do have plenty of cases that meet the standard Coyne is talking about."

"What's the appropriate burden of proof?" I asked. "Many skeptics say extraordinary claims require extraordinary evidence."[2]

"The question is how to define an ambiguous term like 'extraordinary.' Skeptics often set the bar infinitely high. I think we need *sufficient* and *credible* evidence, which varies in each case. The standard needs to be reasonable so that we're not too credulous but we don't rule out things at the outset."

"What standard do you suggest?"

"In civil law, the standard is 'more probable than not.' That's also the standard most historians apply in their work. So I think this is an appropriate benchmark to apply when evaluating miracle claims. Ultimately, of course, people are going to look at events through their own interpretive grid."

"In other words, this really is a worldview issue, isn't it?" I said.

"Certainly. If you give miracles a zero chance of ever occurring, as [skeptic David] Hume did, then you're not going to find any. But if you keep an open mind and follow the evidence wherever it leads—well, it might take you to unexpected places."

14
. . . .

"Following the evidence wherever
it leads" seems wise. Where does
it lead concerning miracles today?

Even after I came to faith, I still retained quite
a bit of skepticism," Dr. Craig Keener told me.
"As a Christian, I believed in miracles in principle,
but I have to admit that I doubted the veracity of
many claims I would hear."

I could certainly relate to that. As a former
newspaper reporter with training in both journalism and law, I used to pride myself in not
taking anything at face value. That skeptical
streak doesn't fade away easily, and I'm sure part
of it never will.

In spite of his doubts, Keener told me he "tried
to maintain intellectual honesty" in his research,
and he followed the facts wherever they led him.
And where did they lead?

"Everywhere I looked, I came across miracle claims that better fit a supernatural explanation than a naturalistic conclusion. Pretty soon, there was an avalanche of examples."

"Such as?"

"Such as . . ." he repeated, as I watched him pause to review years of research and 1,172 pages of information he had written about miracles. Finally, he answered in a sincere but animated fashion.

"Cataracts and goiters—instantly and visibly healed," he said. "Paralytics suddenly able to walk. Multiple sclerosis radically cured. Broken bones suddenly mended. Hearing for the deaf. Sight for the blind. Voices restored. Burns disappearing. Massive hemorrhaging stopped. Failing kidneys cured. Rheumatoid arthritis and osteoporosis—gone. Life given back to the dead, even after several hours.

"I have accounts from around the world—China, Mozambique, the Philippines, Nigeria, Argentina, Brazil, Cuba, Ecuador, Indonesia, South Korea, and other countries. Multiple and independent eyewitnesses with reputations for integrity, including physicians. Names, dates, medical documentation in many cases. There's even a peer-reviewed scientific study confirming the healing of the deaf.

"And the timing is usually the most dramatic element—instantaneous results right after prayers to Jesus. Lots of cancer healings too—malignant brain tumors and reticulum-cell sarcoma, for example—but I didn't include most of those in my book, since I knew people would write them off as spontaneous remissions. Still, when the remission happens so quickly and completely after specific prayers, that's very suspicious."

"And your conclusion from all of this is—what?" I asked.

"That apart from some sort of divine intervention, many of these phenomena seem inexplicable. In other words, a lot of these cases better fit a supernatural explanation than a natural one."

I agree—and couldn't have said it better myself.

15

Why do so many accounts
of miracles come from
faraway places?

That's a challenging question. I can't easily
answer it with chapter-and-verse from the
Bible, yet I think there are biblical teachings that
help us know how to respond.

The first thing I should say, though, is that
there are *many* reports of miracles right here at
home. I mentioned earlier the study I commissioned with Barna Research. The results were
impressive. We found that nearly two out of five
US adults (38 percent) said they believe God has
intervened supernaturally in their lives. And the
more I researched this topic, the more homegrown
stories I heard.

That said, there does seem to be a concentration of miracles being reported in other parts of the world—like divine healings in Mozambique and dreams and visions in the Middle East. Why is that? Here are a few thoughts.

First, God seems to work where he's most needed. We in the West have much greater access to resources like medical supplies, testing equipment, doctors, and hospitals—all of which makes us more self-sufficient. So God seems to focus his activities where people need him most critically.

Second, people in those areas of need are often more diligent in crying out to God for help, and he also tends to go where he's most invited (James 4:2). There's a recurring theme in the Bible that assures us the prayers of God's people reach God's ears, and that he responds to their needs accordingly (see, for example, Psalm 18:6, Psalm 34:15, and James 5:4).

Third, there seems to be an aspect of Jesus' promise concerning the coming Holy Spirit that is relevant: "When he comes, he will prove the world to be in the wrong about sin and righteousness and judgment" (John 16:8). Specifically, Jesus taught that as part of God's evangelistic enterprise he would send his Spirit throughout the world to do what it takes to awaken people to the realities of their sin, to their need for his righteousness, and about the coming judgment.

I believe this includes his working super-naturally in places where it is difficult for us to work naturally—including, yes, places like Mozambique and the Middle East. Perhaps this is at least part of what the Bible means when it talks about God going before us, his people.

God is going to places we can't yet go, doing work we're not yet able to do, and reaching people we're not yet able to reach. And what would moti-vate him to do all of that?

"For God so loved the world."

16

Can God still raise people from the dead today?

On October 20, 2006, a fifty-three-year-old auto mechanic named Jeff Markin walked into the emergency room at Palm Beach Gardens Hospital in Florida, then collapsed from a heart attack. For forty minutes, emergency room personnel frantically labored to revive him, shocking him seven times with the defibrillator, but he was unresponsive.

Finally, the supervising cardiologist, Chauncey Crandall, a well-respected doctor and medical school professor, was brought in to examine the body. Markin's face, toes, and fingers had already turned black from the lack of oxygen. His pupils were dilated and fixed. There was no point in trying to resuscitate him. At 8:05 p.m., he was declared dead.

Crandall filled out the final report and turned to leave. But he quickly felt an extraordinary compulsion. "I sensed God was telling me to turn around and pray for the patient," he said later. This seemed foolish, so he tried to ignore it, only to receive a second—and even stronger—divine prompting.

A nurse was already disconnecting the intravenous fluids and sponging the body so it could be taken to the morgue. But Crandall began praying over the corpse: "Father, God, I cry out for the soul of this man. If he does not know you as his Lord and Savior, please raise him from the dead right now in Jesus' name."

Crandall told the emergency room doctor to use the paddle to shock the corpse one more time. The doctor protested: "I've shocked him again and again. He's dead." But he complied anyway, out of respect for his colleague.

Instantly, the monitor jumped from flat-line to a normal heartbeat of about seventy-five beats per minute with a healthy rhythm. "In my more than twenty years as a cardiologist, I have never seen a heartbeat restored so completely and suddenly," Crandall said.

Markin immediately began breathing without assistance, and the blackness receded from his face, toes, and fingers. The nurse panicked because she feared the patient would be permanently disabled from oxygen deprivation, yet he never displayed any signs of brain damage.[1]

Indeed, in light of the circumstances, natural explanations seem hollow and forced—and they can't account for the two mysterious urges that made Crandall turn in his tracks and pray for a victim who had already been declared dead. Absent those divine promptings, Jeff Markin would be in his grave today.

Can God still raise people from the dead? He can—and sometimes he does!

17

Why don't credible stories of miracles convince skeptics that supernatural events are possible?

That really depends on the skeptic. Is he or she willing to follow the evidence wherever it leads? Or is his or her mind already made up, and therefore impervious to the claims people make—well documented or otherwise?

When I was an atheist, I was certainly resistant to such claims, but thankfully I had just enough openness to try to set aside my biases and look into the evidence. Ultimately it was the evidence for Jesus' resurrection that opened my eyes and turned my life around. But for many skeptics it seems that doubt has become their religion, and they hold to it obstinately, even when the facts militate against them.

For example, Professor Craig Keener told me a

story involving philosopher David Hume and the prominent French scientist and mathematician Blaise Pascal.

"Pascal's niece, Marguerite Perrier, suffered from a severe and long-term fistula in her eye that let out a repulsive odor. At a monastery on March 24, 1656, she was completely healed in a dramatic way, with even bone deterioration vanishing immediately. There was medical and eyewitness evidence; the diocese verified the healing. Even the royal physicians examined her, and the queen herself declared it a healing. In the following months, eighty other miracle claims followed.

"So here you have miracles that were recent, public, attested by many witnesses and even physicians, all of which met Hume's criteria for evidence. But ultimately he dismissed all of this as irrelevant."

"Why?" I asked.

"On the grounds that miracles simply aren't possible because they violate nature," Keener explained.

But that, you see, is the approach of someone

who has already made up his mind and who, therefore, dismisses new evidence out of hand. Philosophers describe this as a "ruling theory"—a presupposition that overshadows and resists anything that seems to contradict it. But once we succumb to that kind of thinking, we're no longer truth-seekers trying to discover what's real. Instead, we've become defenders of a position, even when it becomes increasingly evident that our position is wrong.

So, again, my advice is to try to recognize and set aside our biases and to be lovers of truth, following the facts wherever they lead. And as I think you're seeing, there are more and more facts pointing to a miracle-working God who cares a lot about us. About *you*.

"Then you will know the truth," Jesus said in John 8:32, "and the truth will set you free."

18

How can God hear my prayers—especially when so many other people are praying at the same time?

This seems like an incomprehensible miracle in itself—the idea that God could stay attuned to the concerns of eight billion people in the world, let alone respond to their prayers. A lot of people struggle with this and assume that even if God is super-powerful and wise, surely he's not stooping to hear their petty concerns.

Think again.

According to the Bible—and the experience of countless people around the globe—God is listening, caring, and able to help. In fact, the Bible assures us that he is all-powerful, all-knowing, and everywhere present, and able to comfort us "in all our troubles, so that we can comfort those in any trouble with the comfort we ourselves receive from God" (2 Corinthians 1:4).

Yes, that's mind-blowing. And encouraging, too. I can't explain how God can hear all of our prayers. In fact, I can't even explain how our navigation systems can track all of our cars, remember where we want to go, and tell us when and where to turn, giving us street names and even including advice on which lane to drive in. And that's based on mere human technology. But just *imagine* what the Creator of everything—including our clever little minds—can keep track of!

Here are some promises from the Bible that I hope will encourage you:

> The righteous cry out, and the LORD
>   hears them;
> he delivers them from all their troubles.
> The LORD is close to the brokenhearted
>   and saves those who are crushed in
>   spirit. (Psalm 34:17–18)

Who is like the LORD our God,
    the One who sits enthroned on high,
who stoops down to look
    on the heavens and the earth? (Psalm
    113:5–6)

This is the confidence we have in approaching God:
    that if we ask anything according to his will, he hears us. (1 John 5:14)

God truly is amazing, and he is able to do what seems to us impossible. He is able to hear our prayers, to care about our needs, and to do "immeasurably more than all we ask or imagine, according to his power that is at work within us" (Ephesians 3:20).

So instead of trying to figure out the miraculous potential of prayer, I'd recommend that we simply *pray.*

19

Why doesn't God always answer my prayers and give me what I ask for?

That's a question that almost every praying person asks at one time or another. A lot could be said in response, but I'll offer just a few thoughts on this challenging matter.

First, your prayers could be blocked because your relationship with God isn't where it needs to be. There's a sobering verse in Isaiah 59:2: "Your iniquities have separated you from your God; your sins have hidden his face from you, so that he will not hear." So sometimes people's prayers are blocked because there's a separation between them and the Father, whereas his promises about help and provision are made to those who first trust and follow him.

But there is one prayer he absolutely promises to answer. It is stated in different ways in different places in the Bible. Here are a few examples:

> Have mercy on me, O God,
>   according to your unfailing love;
> according to your great compassion
>   blot out my transgressions.
> Wash away all my iniquity
>   and cleanse me from my sin. (Psalm 51:1–2)

If we confess our sins, he is faithful and just and will forgive us our sins and purify us from all unrighteousness. (1 John 1:9)

If you declare with your mouth, "Jesus is Lord," and believe in your heart that God raised him from the dead, you will be saved. For it is with your heart that you believe and are justified, and it is with your mouth that you profess your faith and are saved. As Scripture says, "Anyone who believes in him

will never be put to shame. . . . [He] is Lord
of all and richly blesses all who call on him."
(Romans 10:9–12)

Second, beyond making sure our relationship
is right with God, we need to be certain we're
actually praying and making our requests known
to him (Philippians 4:6). Wishful thinking is not
the same thing as prayer. Sometimes, as James
4:2 cautions us, "You do not have because you do
not ask God." Also, as the very next verse explains
(v. 3), we need to make sure we're asking from pure
motives as well.

But even when we have these things right, we
still need to leave room for God's wisdom concerning our requests. Sometimes he doesn't give
us what we've asked for because he knows what's
best for us and is willing to disappoint us in order
to better disciple us. As Christian author Tricia
Lott Williford put it, "There's no formula we can
count on for when Jesus says yes and when he says
no. That's the catch with sovereignty: He gets to
decide yes, no, if, when, and how. We can't figure

out what he'll decide, and we can't base our own confidence on his favor. We can, however, base our confidence on his faithfulness."[1]

And, I would add, we can keep praying in the meantime to the God who loves us more than we can even imagine.

20

Haven't studies proven
that prayer doesn't make
any difference?

The Study of the Therapeutic Effects of
Intercessory Prayer (STEP), conducted under
the auspices of the Harvard Medical School, is a
well-known study that seemed to say just that. It
was a ten-year clinical trial of the effects of prayer
on 1,802 cardiac bypass patients at six hospitals—
costing a whopping $2.4 million![1]

The study focused on people who were under-
going cardiac bypass surgery. They were separated
into three groups: one that was prayed for and a
second that was not, though neither of them knew
whether or not they were being prayed for. A third
group was prayed for and was told so. Then the
team kept track of who had complications from
their surgeries.

"The results were very revealing," said skeptic Michael Shermer. "There was no difference in the rate of complications for patients who were prayed for and those who were not. Nothing. Zero. In fact, those who knew they were being prayed for had *more* complications. So when you get beyond anecdotes and use the scientific method, there's no evidence for the miraculous."

Seems sobering, but let's look deeper.

I interviewed a professor of religious studies at Indiana University, Candy Gunther Brown, who earned her doctorate at Harvard and wrote *Testing Prayer: Science and Healing*, published by Harvard University Press. I asked Brown about the STEP study.

"If you're going to study prayer," she replied, "wouldn't it be important who was praying, who they were praying to, and how they were praying?"

It turns out the people doing the praying in that study were members of the so-called Unity School of Christianity in Lee's Summit, Missouri. This is a sect that denies biblical teachings on the divinity of Jesus, sin and salvation, the Trinity, the Bible, and just about every other key Christian doctrine.

What's more, Brown told me, "Unity leaders have long denied that prayer works miracles and have even called petitionary prayers 'useless.'"[2]

So this much-touted study, which seems to discredit the power of prayer, is actually a discredited study of what happens when people who don't believe in prayer mouth "prayers" for others!

"In the end," I asked, "does this study tell us *anything* that's helpful?"

"Well," Brown replied, "it is instructive on how *not* to conduct a study of Christian prayer."

21

Have there been other, more positive studies done on the impact of prayer?

I raised that question with Dr. Candy Gunther Brown, the professor of religious studies at Indiana University, who has focused much of her energy on this very question.

"There have been 'gold standard' studies before and after the [Harvard STEP] study that reached the opposite conclusion: that the group receiving prayer had *better* outcomes," she said.

"Really?" I asked. "Can you give me some examples?"

"One of the first widely publicized studies was by Dr. Randolph Byrd, published in 1988 in the peer-reviewed *Southern Medical Journal*," she said. "It was a prospective, randomized, double-blinded, controlled study of four hundred subjects."

She explained that born-again Christians, both Catholics and Protestants, were given the patient's first name, condition, and diagnosis. They were instructed to pray to the Judeo-Christian God "for a rapid recovery and for prevention of complications and death, in addition to other areas of prayer they believed to be beneficial to patients."

"The results?" I asked.

"Patients in the prayer group had less congestive heart failure, fewer cardiac arrests, fewer episodes of pneumonia, were less often intubated and ventilated, and needed less diuretic and antibiotic therapy," she said.

"That's very interesting," I replied.

"Then a decade or so later," Brown continued, "a replication study by Dr. William S. Harris and colleagues was published in the *Archives of Internal Medicine*."

"Were the results similar?"

"This was a 'gold standard' study of the effects of intercessory prayer on almost a thousand consecutively admitted coronary patients. Half received prayer; the other half didn't. And again, the group that received prayer had better outcomes than the control group."

"So let me get this straight," I said. "These studies affirmed that the recipients of prayer had better outcomes than those who didn't."

Brown nodded. "That's right."

Someone said that bad news travels halfway around the world while good news is still putting on its shoes. Sadly, the negative and flawed STEP study has been heavily publicized and discussed endlessly, while few have even heard about these other studies that reinforce the validity of prayer. I hope you're encouraged to hear these results and that together we can get this good news out to others.

Sincere prayer, when expressed to the true God by people of genuine faith, really does make a difference.

22

Can science really investigate the effects of prayer?

That's another question I asked the professor of religious studies at Indiana University, Candy Gunther Brown.

"In several ways," Brown told me. "For one thing, medical records can be compared before and after prayer occurs. Was there a condition that was diagnosed? Do X-rays, blood tests, or other diagnostic procedures show illness or injury? And then was there some resolution of that condition?"

"Of course, you can't prove God healed them, even if their illness disappears," I interjected.

"Correct. There may have been medical treatment, or the placebo effect may be involved, or a spontaneous remission. Even diagnostic tests can be open to interpretation. Plus, relapses might occur later," she replied. "On the other hand, if there's no improvement or a worsening of their illness, then we can say a miracle cure definitely *didn't* take place. Science is better at disproving things than proving them."

"Clinical studies can be of help too," I offered.

"I believe so. They're set up for a short-term window of time so we can measure what happens after the intervention of prayer. Now, there can be complications, such as people outside the study who are praying for people inside the study, or the application of medical treatment, or subsequent relapses. And, of course, everyone brings their own assumptions when they interpret the data, depending on where they are on the spectrum."

"The spectrum?"

"Yes, on one end of the spectrum are those who expect miracles to be very, very likely. They believe God frequently intervenes in nature. They may be quick to conclude, 'God has healed this person through prayer.' But people on the opposite end of the spectrum start with the assumption that miracles *never* happen. If there's a zero likelihood, then regardless of how strong the evidence is, there has to be a more plausible explanation, right? So there is going to be a pre-conditioning to interpret things depending on where you start off."

The challenge for all of us, I would add, is to admit and attempt to compensate for our own biases in order to stay as open as possible to the evidence of the study. And when we do that, there seems to be quite a bit in the studies to show that dramatic changes sometimes happen, right then and there in the moments during and after people pray for a miracle.

To me, that points toward the reality of a supernatural intervention by God.

23

Are there any keys to praying in ways that lead to supernatural results?

While there are certainly no pat formulas for prayer, here are four biblical essentials worth sharing:

- First, our relationship with God is key. As we discussed earlier, sin in our lives can block our prayers. It's vital that we first trust in Christ as our Forgiver and Leader, so we know we're in a genuine relationship with him. Beyond that, we need to make sure we're not harboring any disobedient patterns in our life, confessing any sin that may have crept in, and keeping the channels of communication and blessings open with God (1 John 1:9). James 5:16 tells us that "the prayer of a *righteous* person is powerful and effective" (emphasis mine).

- Second, we must actually *pray*! I say this because it's so easy for all of us, myself included, to talk about praying for things—and even to ask others to pray for our needs—but then fail to actually make our requests to God. Jesus told us in Matthew 6:6 to "go into your room, close the door and pray to your Father, who is unseen. Then your Father, who sees what is done in secret, will reward you."

- Third, we need to approach God in faith, believing he loves us, he hears our prayers and cares for our needs, and he is able to intervene in surprising and powerful ways. Over and over when Jesus healed people he would explain that his miracle was related to their faith. And how can we increase our faith? Romans 10:17 tells us, "Faith comes from hearing the message, and the message is heard through the word about Christ"—so increased exposure to God's Word can definitely help.

- Fourth, according to Candy Gunther Brown of Indiana University, the prayers that are most effective in bringing healing are usually those in which the people who are praying "get up close to someone they know . . . come in physical contact with them . . . [and] empathize with their sufferings." This makes sense to me, especially since Jesus would generally touch those he healed. Also, James 5:14 tells us to anoint the sick with oil when we pray for them. This obviously involves physical proximity and contact.

Much more could be said, but these are some of the keys to praying in ways that, as James 5:16 puts it, will be "powerful and effective."

24

Does prayer change God's mind? How can prayer make a difference when God already knows the future?

I don't think prayer changes God's mind. But I do think God chooses to respond to the prayers of his people, so in that sense prayer changes *things*.

Now, I know some people claim prayer is only about changing *us*, and I agree that's part of what it does. It helps align us with God's mind and will. But it does more than that. Again, James 5:16 says, "The prayer of a righteous person is powerful and effective," and he gives an example from the life of Elijah. "He prayed earnestly that it would not rain, and it did not rain on the land for three and a half years. Again he prayed, and the heavens gave rain, and the earth produced its crops" (vv. 17–18).

His prayer changed a lot more than the one who was praying!

But, you say, *if God knows everything that's going to happen, then whatever is going to happen has already been locked in—and prayer can't change that!*

I asked my philosophy-trained friend, Mark Mittelberg, how he would respond to this. "What I try to explain," Mark began, "is that the Bible makes it clear that God fully knows ahead of time what we will freely do. So the first point I would make is that God's foreknowledge does not preclude our real freedom."

"Yes," I responded, "but that doesn't answer the question about prayer."

"That's why I have a second point!" Mark replied. "Not only does God know what we will freely do, he also knows what we will freely pray. More than that, he knows how he will respond to those prayers. In fact, when we decide to pray today, we're doing exactly what he knew we would do, and he responds to those prayers, in time, in just the way he knew he should."

"Okay . . ." I began.

"But," Mark continued buoyantly, "if we decide *not* to pray, then the God who knows the future might have already decided not to give us the help we could have had if we had simply prayed. So even though God sees the future, prayer really does make a difference."

"*Philosophers!*" I responded.

I do think that makes sense, though—almost as much sense as Jesus did when he simply told us to pray to our heavenly Father, who "knows what you need before you ask him" (Matthew 6:8).

25

Aren't there a lot of fake miracles?

Undoubtedly so—just as there is a lot of fake jewelry in the world. But that fact doesn't discredit the existence of real diamonds and jewels!

I read an article on the subject of fake miracles in *Skeptic* magazine, edited by my skeptical friend, Michael Shermer. It was titled "On Miracles," and was written by a retired physician named Harriet Hall.[1] Her goal was to refute the possibility of divine activity in the world today. While there was much in the piece that I would dispute, I'll also acknowledge that Hall made some valid points:

- She said that spontaneous remissions occur. *Point granted.*
- She said there are a lot of charlatans in the world. *Absolutely, yes.*

- She said sometimes blood tests are in error, X-rays are misinterpreted, and diagnoses are wrong. *No one would know this better than a doctor.*
- She said coincidences happen. *Without a doubt.*
- She said some people have a motivation to lie. *Certainly.*
- She said even honest people can misjudge things. *Acknowledged.*
- She said memories can falter. *I can attest to that.*
- She said people who are only apparently dead can revive. *Thankfully, yes.*
- She said any quack can supply testimonials that his snake oil works. *Sure.*

All of this is true, but does it explain away all of the accounts of miracles? *Definitely not.*

Believing that miracles sometimes happen does not mean we have to buy into every miraculous story that gets reported in the tabloids or repeated on the Internet. A lot of the time weird stories are merely that: strange phenomena or clever trickery. Sometimes we can explain them and sometimes we can't, but that doesn't discredit every miracle claim.

Hall went on to add that eyewitnesses are "notoriously unreliable." While, yes, there can be problems with eyewitness accounts, I would bet that if one of Hall's relatives were murdered, she would hope for eyewitnesses to testify in court against the assailant.

All her point does is underscore the need to test eyewitness accounts by considering the witness's character, motives, biases, and opportunity to see what occurred, and then to seek corroboration and documentation wherever possible. This is simply standard practice for lawyers, judges, journalists, police detectives, historians, juries, and others who are authentically trying to pursue truth.

Should we investigate claims of the miraculous cautiously? Absolutely! We should do exactly as the Bible tells us: "Examine everything carefully; hold fast to that which is good" (1 Thessalonians 5:21 NASB).

26

Can a miracle be real but not be from God?

My answer is yes—and no. *Yes*, things can happen that are supernatural ("beyond nature") while not being from God. But *no*, these would not be divine miracles as we defined them earlier. That's because they were not "brought about by the power of God," nor would they be "for the purpose of showing that God has acted in history."[1] These are *counterfeit* miracles.

The Bible makes it clear that Satan is a real but evil being who has real, but limited power. Let me give a few examples from Scripture.

Exodus 7:10–12 tells us:

> Moses and Aaron went to Pharaoh and did just as the LORD commanded. Aaron threw his staff down in front of Pharaoh and his

officials, and it became a snake. Pharaoh then summoned wise men and sorcerers, and *the Egyptian magicians also did the same things by their secret arts: Each one threw down his staff and it became a snake* (emphasis mine).

These were not magic tricks. These sorcerers were tapping real power, even though it was against God and his purposes.

In the New Testament, Acts 16:16 describes a woman who "had a spirit by which she predicted the future." Where did she get this power? From a demon that indwelled her—the one that Paul ultimately drove out of her (v. 18).

In Mark 5:4 we read about a man who "had often been chained hand and foot, but he tore the chains apart and broke the irons on his feet. No one was strong enough to subdue him." Again, he got his power from an evil spirit—one that Jesus cast out.

Paul warned about a coming false prophet who "will use all sorts of displays of power through signs and wonders that serve the lie, and all the ways that wickedness deceives those who are perishing" (2 Thessalonians 2:9–10).

Jesus warned that "false messiahs and false prophets will appear and perform great signs and wonders to deceive, if possible, even the elect. See, I have told you ahead of time" (Matthew 24:24–25).

So if Satan can imitate God's power, how can we know the difference? Jesus said, "Watch out for false prophets. They come to you in sheep's clothing, but inwardly they are ferocious wolves. *By their fruit you will recognize them*" (Matthew 7:15–16, emphasis mine).

And what is that fruit? It's the life they live, the impact they have, and the message they bring. God's true miracles flow from godly people who have a godly influence, and who bring a consistently faithful, biblical message.

27

How did the critics of Jesus respond to his miracles?

That depended on their level of openness and the condition of their hearts. For those who were open, they were willing to follow Jesus' advice when he said, "even though you do not believe me, believe the works, that you may know and understand that the Father is in me, and I in the Father" (John 10:38). But those who stayed closed would "suppress the truth by their wickedness" (Romans 1:18) and ultimately "perish because they refused to love the truth and so be saved" (2 Thessalonians 2:10).

Let's look at examples of both responses, starting with those who were closed.

On another Sabbath he went into the synagogue and was teaching, and a man was there whose right hand was shriveled. The Pharisees and the teachers of the law were looking for a reason to accuse Jesus, so they watched him closely to see if he would heal on the Sabbath. But Jesus knew what they were thinking and said to the man with the shriveled hand, "Get up and stand in front of everyone." So he got up and stood there.

Then Jesus said to them, "I ask you, which is lawful on the Sabbath: to do good or to do evil, to save life or to destroy it?"

He looked around at them all, and then said to the man, "Stretch out your hand." He did so, and his hand was completely restored. But the Pharisees and the teachers of the law were furious and began to discuss with one another what they might do to Jesus. (Luke 6:6–11)

Just think about this. Jesus performed an extraordinary act of power and grace—he healed this man right before their eyes. And their response? They didn't deny the miracle, but they tried to disqualify Jesus because, according to their legalistic rules, he did it on the wrong day. Talk about hard hearts!

Thankfully, others were more open. Here's the response of Saul (who became Paul) to God's supernatural work.

Meanwhile, Saul was still breathing out murderous threats against the Lord's disciples. He went to the high priest and asked him for letters to the synagogues in Damascus, so that if he found any there who belonged to the Way, whether men or women, he might take them as prisoners to Jerusalem. As he neared Damascus on his journey, suddenly a light from heaven flashed around him. He fell to the ground and heard a voice say to him, "Saul, Saul, why do you persecute me?"

"Who are you, Lord?" Saul asked.

"I am Jesus, whom you are persecuting," he replied. "Now get up and go into the city, and you will be told what you must do." (Acts 9:1–6)

So then . . . [Paul wrote,] I was not disobedient to the vision from heaven. First to those in Damascus, then to those in Jerusalem and in all Judea, and then to the Gentiles, I preached that they should repent and turn to God and demonstrate their repentance by their deeds. (Acts 26:19–20)

The challenge is for people—*for us*—to do what Paul did. We need to set aside our biases and prejudices, to humble our spirits and open our hearts, and to let God's work impact us at the deepest of levels. When we do this, Jesus' miracles will draw us to Jesus' magnificent salvation.

28

Can God heal a broken heart?

If you mean a heart that's been hurt or abandoned, then there's nobody better to turn to than the One who created your heart in the first place. "A father to the fatherless, a defender of widows, is God in his holy dwelling. God sets the lonely in families, he leads out the prisoners with singing" (Psalm 68:5–6). And he promises "to proclaim good news to the poor . . . to bind up the brokenhearted, to proclaim freedom for the captives and release from darkness for the prisoners . . . to comfort all who mourn" (Isaiah 61:1–2).

And Jesus, who embodied these attributes described by Isaiah (see Luke 4:18–21), also warned, "In this world you will have trouble. But take heart! I have overcome the world" (John 16:33).

In my book *The Case for Grace* I recount story after story of hurting people with broken hearts whose lives were supernaturally transformed by the work of our grace-giving, miracle-working God. I tell of a drug addict who didn't care if he lived or died—but who was reclaimed by God. Today he lives a full and rewarding life as the pastor of one of the most dynamic churches in America.

I describe how a homeless man was hopeless beyond repair were it not for the miraculous intervention of a God who showed love to him through his followers—people from the former drug addict's church who had a vision for rescuing men and women from the streets. Today that man is married to a wonderful woman (who had helped feed him when he was starving), and he tells his story around the country, proclaiming God's ability to salvage a seemingly lost life and turn it into something beautiful.

I also tell the story of a pastor friend who briefly fell into adultery. He lost his ministry and almost lost his wife, and he was afraid he would never be able to serve the Lord again. But God healed Brad's broken heart, along with his wife's, and today they have a thriving marriage and family. In fact, they now write, speak, and lead conferences—all designed to help other couples build their marriages into all that God intended for them.[1]

Me? Leslie and I have lived through the losses of our parents as well as other relatives and friends. As followers of Christ we grieved deeply each time—but not as those "who have no hope," as 1 Thessalonians 4:13 explains.

So, yes, I believe that in spite of all you're going through, God can perform an astounding miracle—he can heal your broken heart. If you'll do what James 4:8 (NKJV) says: "Draw near to God," then "He will draw near to you."

29

What about a physical heart— can God heal that too?

Ed Wilkinson was a Christian whose education in neuropsychology convinced him that people who rely on faith to cure their ills are merely using religion as a neurosis to avoid dealing with reality. He soon found his views put to the test.

"In November 1984, [Ed's] eight-year-old son, Brad, was diagnosed with two holes in his heart. The condition also impaired his lungs. Surgery was scheduled," said Craig Keener, author of *Miracles*. "As the surgery got closer, Brad started giving away his toys, not expecting he would survive. One day he asked his dad, 'Am I going to die?'"

Ed told him, "Not everyone who has heart surgery dies, but it can happen.' Then his son asked, 'Can Jesus heal me?'

"He said he needed to think about that one.

"A few days later," Keener continued, "after some anguished prayers and reading Philippians 4:13,[1] Ed told him that God does heal, but whether he would in Brad's case or not, they still had hope of eternal life in Jesus.

"After that, a visiting pastor asked Brad, 'Do you believe that Jesus can heal you?' Brad said yes, and the minister prayed for him."[2]

Before surgery at the University of Missouri hospital in Columbia, Missouri, tests confirmed nothing had changed with Brad's condition. The following morning, Brad was taken in for his operation, which was expected to last four hours. But after an hour, the surgeon summoned Ed and showed him two films.

The first film, taken the prior day, showed blood leaking from one heart chamber to another. The second film, taken just as surgery started, showed a wall of some sort where the leak had been. The surgeon said there was now nothing wrong with Brad's heart, even though the holes were clearly visible the day before. The lungs were also now normal.

The doctor explained that a spontaneous closure rarely happens in infants, but it was not supposed to occur in an eight-year-old. "You can count this as a miracle," he said.

The hospital risk manager said firmly: "You can see from the films: this was *not* a misdiagnosis." Added the pulmonologist: "Somebody somewhere must have been praying."

Today Brad is in his thirties with a business and children of his own. He has never had any heart problems since his healing.

30

What would you say to a cessationist—a Christian who doesn't believe miracles still happen today?

First, to be fair, not all Christians who hold to a cessationist view would deny that God sometimes does miracles today. "There are two kinds of cessationists," theologian Roger Olson explains. "One kind says God no longer offers a *spiritual gift* of healing; the other kind says *miracles themselves* have ceased."

Those in both camps tend to view miracles as signs that were primarily given by God during certain periods in biblical history to establish his work during that era—most recently during the time of Jesus and the apostles. And certainly God has used miracles in that way.

Some would also cite 1 Corinthians 13:8–10: "Where there are prophecies, they will cease; where there are tongues, they will be stilled; where there is knowledge, it will pass away. For we know in part and we prophesy in part, but when completeness comes, what is in part disappears." They view the "completeness" there as the establishment of the canon of Scripture at the end of the apostolic era. This, they would say, marked the end of such miraculous activities.

My take on this? I don't embrace cessationism, and I think the "completeness" in the 1 Corinthians 13 passage probably refers to the time when Christ will return to renew all things. And while I'm cautious about those who claim to have spiritual gifts in areas like prophecy, healing, and miracles, I don't deny that these could be authentic (see 1 Thessalonians 5:19–22).

My main challenge would be to those who categorically deny that miracles can happen today. I'm convinced this view goes against the strong evidence we see for supernatural events all around us, and, more importantly, that such a position is unsupported by the Bible. Peter declared on the day of Pentecost:

> "In the last days, God says,
>   I will pour out my Spirit on all people.
> Your sons and daughters will prophesy,
>   your young men will see visions,
> your old men will dream dreams.
>   Even on my servants, both men and
>   women,
> I will pour out my Spirit in those days,
>   and they will prophesy.
> I will show wonders in the heavens above
>   and signs on the earth below,
> blood and fire and billows of smoke.
>   The sun will be turned to darkness
> and the moon to blood
>   before the coming of the great and
>   glorious day of the Lord.
> And everyone who calls
>   on the name of the Lord will be
>   saved." (Acts 2:17–21)

Finally, I agree with pastor John Piper when he says, "I want to have my keel deep and stable in the once-for-all biblical revelation of God, and I want to have my sails unfurled to every movement of God's Spirit upon the deeps."[1]

31

Why trust the biblical accounts of Jesus' miracles? Weren't the writers biased, since they were already believers?

I have to challenge the "already" part of the question.

I'm not disputing the fact that the New Testament writers who testified to the miracles and resurrection of Jesus were true believers; the question is how they *became* believers.

Peter was a fisherman—a group not known for wandering away from their boats to follow religious teachers. They had, after all, heard "fish stories" all their lives and could readily see through them. Yet when Peter was called by Jesus, he immediately left his nets and followed him (see Mark 1:16–18, where Peter was referred to as Simon). This was the beginning of three years of daily interaction with Jesus, observation of his miracles, and eventually seeing him crucified on a cross and then return alive again three days later.

No wonder Peter later explained, "We did not follow cleverly devised stories when we told you about the coming of our Lord Jesus Christ in power, but we were eyewitnesses of his majesty" (2 Peter 1:16). Peter told us what he saw in his epistles, 1 Peter and 2 Peter, as well as in the Gospel of Mark, which history indicates was based on Peter's account, though recorded by Mark.[1]

Matthew was a tax collector—a generally despised but wealthy group of people who were not known for walking away from their lucrative practices to follow alleged messiahs. Yet that's exactly what Matthew did (see Mark 2:13–14, where he is called Levi)—and then he later wrote down what he had experienced as a follower of Jesus in the first book of the New Testament, the Gospel of Matthew.

And Paul? How do you explain a zealous Jewish leader, whose goal was to destroy the church (Acts 8:3), turning around to become the world's greatest missionary *for* the church? Was he biased—or simply persuaded, as he claimed, by seeing the risen Savior (Acts 9:1–31)?

Other examples could be given, but these should make the point: the New Testament writers merely reported what they had witnessed. They became believers *because* of what they had seen and heard (see 1 John 1:1–4).

As my ministry partner Mark Mittelberg often explains when we teach together, "Dismissing the writers of Scripture for believing what they had seen and heard would be like ignoring all of the eyewitnesses in a legal trial because they were convinced that what they had witnessed really happened!"

32

Does believing in the evidence for miracles compete with simple faith in God?

Atheist Richard Dawkins famously declared: "Faith is belief in spite of, even perhaps because of, the lack of evidence."[1]

Now, I don't think I've ever met a Christian who would say he or she believes in Christ in the complete absence of knowledge, evidence, or experience of God. And I certainly disagree with those who say we have to take a blind leap of faith in order to follow Jesus.

I think biblical faith is expressed by taking a step in the same direction that the evidence points. The best synonym for faith is *trust*—and we should always put our trust in things that have proven to be *trustworthy*. So we test ideas to see if they make sense—that they are logical and clear. We look for evidence that what we're considering believing is really true.

And in the case of Christianity, where we're putting our faith in a supernatural God, it's natural to ask whether he has performed supernatural works. So when we see credible evidence that God has done miracles—or when he does one in our own life—that obviously becomes another reason to put our trust in him.

Therefore logic, evidence, and miracles can combine to help us know Christian beliefs are trustworthy and thus encourage us to put our trust—*our faith*—in Christ.

Let me illustrate this with the example of my late friend, Nabeel Qureshi. Nabeel grew up in a wonderful and loving American Muslim family. He wholeheartedly practiced his faith and was excited to share Islam with everyone he met. Then he met David Wood, a recent follower of Christ.

Nabeel and David became fast friends who passionately shared their respective faiths with each other. Over time, as Nabeel studied both the Islamic and Christian sources, he reluctantly became convinced that the evidence pointed to the truth of Christianity. But knowing the pain it would cause his family if he decided to follow Jesus, Nabeel cried out to Allah—or whoever the true God is—to speak to him in a supernatural way.

God answered Nabeel's prayers, soon giving him a vision and three dreams, all of which convinced him conclusively that God was speaking to him in a supernatural way, and that he needed to put his trust in Christ. Nabeel told his story in his powerful book, *Seeking Allah, Finding Jesus*, which I highly recommend.[2]

For Nabeel, as for many others, miracles confirmed the information gained through reading and research—and ultimately helped pave the way to faith in Jesus. The evidence became a catalyst for true faith—not a competitor.

33

How did your Muslim friend know that his dreams were from God?

It's not surprising that a Muslim who is intently studying Christianity might have a dream or two about it. But for Nabeel Qureshi, author of *Seeking Allah, Finding Jesus*, it went much further than ordinary dreams. Here's how he described one of them to me.

> The brick wall was faded, uneven and weathered; the imposing wooden door was more than seven feet tall but less than three feet wide, arched at its top and situated in a doorway that was a few feet deep.
>
> The visitor stood outside in the darkness, peering into the warm glow of the baroque

interior—a cavernous room filled with tables overflowing with sumptuous food and chalices of wine. The people inside were ready to enjoy their feast, but they were all waiting as they looked to their left, as if anticipating someone was going to speak before the meal.

Peering in, the visitor saw his friend, David, sitting at a table not far from the doorway. Surprised, he called to get David's attention. "I thought we were going to eat together," the visitor called out.

David, his gaze never leaving the front of the room, was only able to reply: "You never responded."

"That was the whole dream," Nabeel told me.

"And this came after you had asked God for a clear vision?" I asked.

"That's right," he replied. "I called David the next day and asked him what he thought of my dream."

David Wood was Nabeel's Christian friend. "And what did he tell you?"

"He said there was no need to interpret what I had experienced. All I needed to do was open the Bible to the thirteenth chapter of Luke."

Then Jesus went through the towns and villages, teaching as he made his way to Jerusalem. Someone asked him, "Lord, are only a few people going to be saved?"

He said to them, "Make every effort to enter through the narrow door, because many, I tell you, will try to enter and will not be able to. Once the owner of the house gets up and closes the door, you will stand outside knocking and pleading, 'Sir, open the door for us.'

"But he will answer, 'I don't know you or where you come from.' . . .

"There will be weeping there, and gnashing of teeth, when you see Abraham, Isaac and Jacob and all the prophets in the kingdom of God, but you yourselves thrown out. People will come from east and west and north and south, and will take their places at the feast in the kingdom of God."[1] (vv. 22–29)

"I was standing at the door and it had not yet closed, but it was clear I would not be at this banquet of God—*this heaven*—unless I responded to the invitation," Nabeel said. "The door would be shut for good; the feast would go on without me, forever."

"That passage in Luke—how many times had you read it before that night?"

"Not once," he replied, surprised I'd asked. "I had never read *any* of the New Testament before—and yet I saw that passage played out in my dream."

"How do you account for that?"

"I'm a man of science. A medical doctor. I deal with flesh and bones, with evidence and facts and logic. But *this*," he said, searching for the right words, "this was the exact vision I needed. It was a miracle. A miracle that opened the door for me."

34

Why do you think so many Muslims are having dreams about Jesus?

Jesus told us to "go and make disciples of all nations" (Matthew 28:19). But in places where it's extraordinarily difficult for us to bring the good news of Christ, he sometimes goes before us in extraordinary ways. That seems to be the case in many Muslim areas that are closed to Christian missionaries. It's as if God is saying, "These people matter too much to me to leave them in spiritual darkness, so I'll find a way to reach them directly."

Christian apologist Ravi Zacharias brought this phenomenon to my attention when I interviewed him for my book *The Case for Faith*.

"I have spoken in many Islamic countries, where it's tough to talk about Jesus," he told me.

"Virtually every Muslim who has come to follow Christ has done so, first, because of the love of Christ expressed through a Christian, or second, because of a vision, dream, or some other supernatural intervention." He added, "No religion has a more intricate doctrine of angels and visions than Islam, and I think it's extraordinary that God uses that sensitivity to the supernatural world in which he speaks in visions and dreams and reveals himself."[1]

In the Bible God frequently used dreams and visions to further his plans. From Abraham, Joseph, and Samuel in the Old Testament to Zacharias, John, and Cornelius in the New Testament, there are about two hundred biblical examples of God employing this kind of divine intervention.

Reports of these miraculous manifestations are now so common in Muslim areas that author and pastor Tom Doyle told me, "I could pick up the phone right now and call Syria and ask if our people have any stories about dreams, and they would give me three or four new ones. That's how prevalent they are."

But prevalent or not, "these are earth-shattering experiences to those who have them," Doyle told me. "They're not like typical dreams—they're exceptionally vibrant. They can't shake them. They sense this love that has been missing from their life—and their response is very understandable: they inevitably want more."

As a result, more Muslims have become Christians in the last couple of decades than in the previous fourteen hundred years since Muhammad lived, and it's estimated that a quarter to a third of them experienced a dream or vision of Jesus before their salvation experience.[2]

35

Can you give examples of dreams and visions impacting Muslims even in the Middle East?

Recently I met a guy in Jerusalem who grew up in a refugee camp as a Palestinian," Tom Doyle, author of *Dreams and Visions*, told me. "He hated Israel. He told me his goal in life was to kill as many Jews as he could."

"So what happened?"

"He was on his way to meet with people who work with Hamas," Doyle said, referring to the terrorist organization. "He didn't know anything about Jesus, but all of a sudden a man in a white robe was standing in front of him in the street and pointing at him. The man said, 'Omar, this is not the life I have planned for you. You turn around. Go home. I have another plan for you.'"

"What did he do?"

"He turned around and went home. Later that same day, someone was moving into an apartment across the hall from him. He found out the new tenant was a Christian. Omar told him about the experience he had and said, 'What does it mean?' This Christian spent time with him, took him through the Scriptures, and led him to Jesus. Today Omar is an underground church planter."

I was just getting my arms around that story when Doyle launched into another.

"We met another guy in Jericho who was part of the Palestinian Authority. He started having dreams about Jesus. He went to his imam, who told him to read the Qur'an more. But the more he read the Qur'an, the more he had Jesus dreams. The imam told him to get more involved in the mosque, so he did—still, more Jesus dreams. The imam said to make the *hajj* to Mecca."

One of the five pillars of Islam says that any Muslim who is able to should make the *hajj*, or pilgrimage to Mecca, once in his lifetime and walk seven times around the *Kaaba*—"The house of Allah"—a black building in the center of the most sacred mosque in Islam. More than a million people walk counterclockwise around the *Kaaba* during this five-day period.

"What happened to him?" I asked.

"You're supposed to look at the *Kaaba* and say your prayers. Instead, he looked over—and on top of the *Kaaba* he saw the Jesus from his dreams. Jesus was looking at him and saying, 'Osama, leave this place. You're going in the wrong direction. Leave and go home.' So he did. Later a Christian friend shared the gospel with him, and he came to faith in Christ. Today this man has such love for Jesus that you can literally see it on his face."

36

Is this Muslim dream
phenomenon limited
to the Middle East?

Missiologist Nik Ripken, author of *The Insanity of God: A True Story of Faith Resurrected*, tells of Muslims experiencing Jesus dreams in various places around the world, including in a small Muslim border town in Central Asia that he sensed God leading him to visit. He had been invited by a European Christian doctor who was working there, but as soon as he arrived at the tiny airport, both he and the doctor were frightened to realize there were five men in traditional Muslim garb also waiting for Nik to arrive—and neither Nik nor the doctor knew these men.

Wanting to avoid the deadly religious persecution so prevalent in that area, the doctor immediately departed, leaving Nik to contend alone with the five strangers. Nik tried to evade them, hoping he could quickly get away on the next flight out, but they tenaciously pursued him through the airport. Finally one said to him in broken English, "We are followers of Jesus." Sensing their sincerity, Nik decided to go with them to talk at a nearby apartment. Here is his account.

One of the five men told me, "I dreamed about a blue book. I was driven, consumed really, by the message of the dream. 'Look for this book,' the dream said, 'read this Bible!' I began a secret search, but I could not find a book like that anywhere in my country. Then, one day, I walked into a Quranic book shop and saw this sea of green books lining the walls. I noticed a book of a different color on a shelf in the back of the store, so I walked back there and pulled out a thick blue volume to discover that it was a Bible. It was published in my own national language. I actually bought a Bible in the Islamic bookstore, took it home, and read it five times. That's how I came to know Jesus."

Another one told me, "I dreamed about finding Jesus, but I didn't even know how or where to look. Then one day I was walking through the market when a man I had never seen before came up to me in the crowd. He said, 'The Holy Spirit told me to give you this book.' He handed me a Bible and disappeared into the crowd. I never saw him again. But I read the Bible he gave me three times from cover to cover, and that's how I came to know and follow Jesus."

Each of these five men told me a different variation of the same story. Each of them had come across a Bible in some unusual, miraculous way. Each one had read the Gospel story of Jesus. Each one had decided to follow Him.[1]

You might be wondering how these five men knew to go to the airport when Nik was arriving that day. Well, they had been praying in the apartment at one thirty that morning and, they explained, "The Holy Spirit told us to go to the airport [and] to go to the first white man who got off

the plane. . . . He was sending this man to answer our questions."[2]

So, yes, this is a phenomenon happening all around the world!

37

Aren't the people having
these dreams religious types
who are predisposed to
experiencing such things?

The skeptical side of me wondered the same
thing, so I asked Middle East missionary and
author Tom Doyle about this.

"No way," he said. "Many live in closed countries where they have no prior exposure to images
or ideas about the Jesus of the Bible. When Jesus
tells them he died for them, that's alien to everything they've learned."

"What does the Qur'an tell them about Jesus?"
I asked.

"That he's a prophet, but most significantly,
the Qur'an says Jesus didn't die on the cross, that
Allah does not have a son, and that nobody can

bear the sins of another. So the very things that Christianity says are essential to faith are explicitly denied in Islamic teachings."

"And so this makes Muslims resistant when you try to initiate a conversation about faith," I said.

"Yes, exactly. A Muslim typically responds by saying the Bible has been corrupted, or Christians worship three gods, or look what happened during the Crusades," Doyle replied. "These are some of the big boulders on the path between them and the real Jesus. But in these high-definition Jesus dreams, they're gently walked around those boulders. They see Jesus for who he is and now they're motivated to learn more.

"It's interesting," he continued, "that after having a dream or vision, the typical objections that Muslims raise against Christianity disappear. I've never met someone who had a Jesus dream who is still hung up on the deity of Christ or the veracity of the Scriptures. Instantly, they know this: Jesus is more than just a prophet. And they want to know more about him."

"It seems that people don't go to sleep Muslims, have a Jesus dream, and then wake up as Christians," I offered.

"That's right, I've never heard of that happening," Doyle replied. "Usually, the dream points them toward someone who can teach them from the Bible and present the gospel—like Omar, who was deterred from meeting with Hamas, went home, and 'coincidentally' found a Christian moving in across the hall," he said, putting the word "coincidentally" in air quotes. "The dreams motivate them to seek the real Jesus and to find the truth in Scripture."

Doyle added, "They're honored Jesus would appear to them. They feel love, grace, safety, protection, affirmation, joy, peace—all these emotions they don't receive from Islam. It rocks their world!"

38

Do these dreams really change people's lives, or are they just passing curiosities?

That's an important issue, which is why I discussed it with author Tom Doyle.

"No question—these dreams generally lead to radical life-change," Doyle told me. "A Muslim who comes to faith in the Middle East is exposing himself to possible rejection, beatings, imprisonment, or even death. This isn't for the faint of heart. This isn't casual Christianity."

This is actually the case wherever a Muslim might live. Nabeel Qureshi explained in his book *Seeking Allah, Finding Jesus*:

> These kinds of killings are not limited to the Middle East. A few months after graduation,

I received a phone call . . . telling me about an entire family of Middle Eastern Christians who had just been slaughtered in New Jersey for bringing dishonor to Islam . . . [but] that was the least of my worries. My family would never do such a thing. . . . The greatest concern for me, were I to accept Jesus as Lord, was that I might be wrong. What if Jesus is not God? I'd be worshiping a human. That would incur the wrath of Allah, and more than anything else, it would secure my abode in hell.

Of course, that is exactly what the Quran teaches. In Islam, there is only one unforgivable sin, *shirk*, the belief that someone other than Allah is God. Shirk is specifically discussed in the context of Jesus in 5:72. He who believes Jesus is God, "Allah has forbidden Heaven for him, and his abode will be the Hellfire."

These are the costs Muslims must calculate when considering the gospel: losing the relationships they have built in this life, potentially losing this life itself, and if they are wrong, losing their afterlife in paradise. It is no understatement to say that Muslims often risk everything to embrace the cross.[1]

"It's ironic," I said to Doyle, "that in America, we see a proliferation of shallow commitments to Christ because of a cultural Christianity that hasn't really revolutionized the person's soul, and yet we're skeptical of how authentic these conversions are in the Middle East, where people face persecution if they pursue their faith."

Doyle agreed. "Before praying with someone to receive Christ, many leaders in the Middle East will ask two questions. First, are you willing to suffer for Jesus? And second, are you willing to die for Jesus?" he said. "I wish we had those two questions in the new members classes at churches in America."

"It might thin the ranks a bit," I mused.

"Probably. But even though these Muslims know that following Jesus could very well lead to rejection by their family or even death, they're coming to faith in unprecedented numbers."

So, yes, I think the typical fruit of these dreams—including those Nabeel Qureshi experienced—is genuine life-change. Tom Doyle's research and writings confirm this a thousand times over.

39

Has God ever used a dream in your life?

Of the countless dreams I had growing up, I only brought the memory of one into my adult life. That's probably because it was the most dramatic and mysterious dream of my early years. It wasn't a dream about Jesus, but one in which I interacted with an angel—and was given a prediction that was fulfilled years later.

It was when I was about twelve years old, prior to my subsequent move into atheism, that I dreamed I was making myself a sandwich in the kitchen. Suddenly a luminous angel appeared and started to explain to me—almost in an offhanded manner—how wonderful and glorious heaven is. I listened, and then I commented nonchalantly, "I'm going there"—meaning at the end of my life.

"How do you know?" came the angel's unsettling reply.

How did I know? What kind of question is that? "Well, uh, I've tried to be a good kid," I stammered. "I've tried to do what my parents say. I've tried to behave. I've been to church."

"That doesn't matter," said the angel abruptly.

I was stunned. How could those things not matter—all my efforts to obey the rules, to be respectful, to live up to the standards set by my parents and teachers? A sense of panic came over me. I couldn't open my mouth to respond.

The angel let me wrestle with my thoughts and then finally said, "Someday you'll understand." Instantly, he was gone—and I woke up in a sweat. This was the only childhood dream I've never forgotten.

In the ensuing years I rejected the possibility of miracles and even God's existence, living as a skeptic for a long period of time. But then some sixteen years after that dream, the angel's prophecy came true.

At Leslie's prompting I visited her church, which was meeting in a movie theater in Palatine, Illinois, and there I heard the message of God's amazing grace. I finally came to understand I couldn't get to heaven by complying with the rules or doing good deeds—it was only by asking Christ to be my Forgiver and Leader that I could receive the free gift of God's salvation.

As soon as I realized this, the memory of that dream came back into my mind, with the angel who had predicted that someday I would understand the gospel. I didn't respond to God's grace right away, but ultimately, it changed my life and my eternity.

Was my dream miraculous? I'll leave it to you to decide. But for me, the results certainly seem supernatural.

40

Have you personally seen someone else's life impacted by a dream from God?

Something fascinating happened at the church where I'm a teaching pastor. The story involves Rachel. She and her husband have a child, and they live in a Houston suburb where I doubt her friends can fathom her upbringing as a devout Muslim in a country where Christianity is forbidden.

When Rachel was younger she was going through a difficult time, so one night she begged God, "Please send me one of your prophets who will release me from this miserable feeling. I badly need comfort and guidance."

That night she had a dream of being in a movie theater where the projector cast a very bright light. Suddenly, there was Jesus. "He was looking at me with very kind, concerned eyes," she said. "It was as if he could feel my pain and my sadness."

Jesus spoke to her, but the words weren't as important as the emotion they evoked: a deep and profound sense of relief, comfort, affirmation, and joy. "My eyes opened but I was sure that I was never asleep," she said. "I was in that room with him."

Several years later, Rachel got married and moved with her husband to Texas. One day she surprised herself by blurting out to a neighbor, "I would like to study the Bible." She ended up studying the Gospel of John with a woman from our church.

As she began the study—and before she knew anything about baptism—she had a vision. "I saw a man with a book," she said. "I was standing with him in water. I saw my friend holding my arm, and we were both looking at the man with the book open in his hands. The man was looking into the horizon with tears running down his face, and I knew that this man loves Jesus very much." She had never seen the man before.

Easter came, and her friend brought her to our church. As they sat waiting for the service to begin, something caught Rachel's attention.

"Over there—that's the man!" she exclaimed. It was the man from her vision—a pastor named Alan Splawn, who presides over baptisms at our church. She had never met him before, but there he was, right in front of her.

Soon Rachel had put her trust in Jesus—a joyous occasion in her life, but not one she dared to share with her husband.

So a private baptism was arranged. "We all went into the baptismal pool," she said. There they were: the man who loves Jesus, reading from an open Bible, and her friend at her side—just as foretold in her vision.

Rachel will never be the same—nor will any of us who saw how God worked in her life.

41

Have you ever heard
God speak to you?

I've never heard an audible voice from God,
though some people have. For me it's usually
more of an impression—sometimes vague, but
occasionally very strong. I mentioned earlier the
time Leslie and I had the distinct impression that
we should send an anonymous five-hundred-dollar
check to a young woman in our church, only to find
out later it was the amount she needed to repair
her car from a breakdown—one that occurred *after*
we had mailed the check. That certainly seemed to
be a prompting from God.

There was also a time when my ministry partner Mark Mittelberg and I were preparing for an
open-mic question-and-answer session at a church
in Atlanta. That night hundreds of participants

would ask us questions about the evidence for Christianity.

As I was getting ready, I felt a strong impression that God wanted me to study up on a question about Mithras, a pagan god who people claim was worshiped long before Jesus, was born of a virgin, was a great traveling teacher, sacrificed himself for world peace, and was resurrected from the dead after three days in a tomb. This myth supposedly influenced the story of Christianity.

I spent several hours focused on this issue. I called an expert on the topic and scoured scholarly articles. As I suspected, the plagiarism charge was grossly inaccurate. According to the actual story, Mithras wasn't born of a virgin but emerged fully grown from a rock; he wasn't a traveling teacher but a mythological god; he didn't sacrifice himself but instead was famous for slaying a bull; and there were no beliefs about his death and hence no resurrection. Besides, Mithraism didn't emerge as a mystery religion until after Christianity had been established. I went to the event that night excited to use the information I'd discovered.

Yet the question never came up. I was puzzled. The impression in my spirit had been so strong that God wanted me to get ready to deal with this issue. *I guess I was misreading things,* I mused.

Two weeks later Mark and I led a similar event at a church in Chicago. It went great, and as we were about to close we decided to take one more question—and it turned out to be from a man who wanted to know if the story about Mithras had influenced Christian beliefs!

I finally had the chance to unload the information God had prompted me to learn. It seemed to encourage the man, and as he was sitting down I heard him say, "That was the last barrier between me and God." Before the night was over, he had prayed to receive Christ as his Forgiver and Leader.

42

If God wants more followers, why doesn't he just do more miracles in order to convince everyone?

This question relates to what is classically referred to as the "hiddenness of God." Why doesn't God just come out into the open and show himself more clearly, knowing that as a result more people would believe in him?

The answer seems to be that, on the one hand, God wants to give people enough evidence to believe in him—but only if they'll pursue him wholeheartedly. Jesus said in Matthew 7:7, "Ask and it will be given to you; seek and you will find; knock and the door will be opened to you." Jeremiah 29:13 adds another element: "You will seek me and find me *when you seek me with all your heart*" (emphasis mine).

So God wants our pursuit of him to be a priority. Jesus explained, "The kingdom of heaven is like a merchant looking for fine pearls. When he found one of great value, he went away and sold everything he had and bought it" (Matthew 13:45–46).

More specifically, Romans 1:19–20 tells us, "What may be known about God is plain to them, because God has made it plain to them. For since the creation of the world God's invisible qualities—his eternal power and divine nature—have been clearly seen, being understood from what has been made, so that people are without excuse."

On the other hand, God seems to avoid making his presence so clear that he overwhelms us and removes our ability to resist him if we wish to. Going back to the passage in Romans, God leaves us with the freedom to choose to continue to "suppress the truth" through our wickedness (Romans 1:18), in spite of all the evidence he gives us.

God wants us to love him, but love can never be forced. So God gives us enough information to see that he's a good God who is worthy of our trust and worship, but not so much that we'll be coerced into following him against our will.

Christian philosopher Blaise Pascal summed it up well when he explained:

> Willing to appear openly to those who seek him with all their heart, and to be hidden from those who flee from him with all their heart, God so regulates the knowledge of himself that he has given indications of himself, which are visible to those who seek him and not to those who do not seek him. There is enough light for those to see who only desire to see, and enough obscurity for those who have a contrary disposition.[1]

THE MIRACLES ANSWER BOOK

43

How can I believe in something that I've never seen or experienced myself?

It's a common refrain: "I'll believe it when I see it!" But there are many ways we come to believe things, only one of which is through personal experience. While that may be the most direct way to learn, you might be surprised to realize how much you believe apart from it.

For example, do you believe in history? I assume you do—but you weren't there to experience much of it. Everything we know about ancient Greece, the Roman Empire, medieval times, the Reformation, and the founding of America comes to us by way of historical writings—the testimonies of those who observed and recorded events of the past—and through archaeological discoveries.

What about science? You believe in protons, neutrons, and electrons, but you've never seen an atom. You believe in DNA, but I doubt you've ever seen a double helix coil. Most of what we know about the microscopic world, as well as about outer space, comes from the findings and testimonies of experts in those fields.

And medicine? We follow the wisdom of the doctor when we take antibiotics (which operate at a level we can't see) to fight a bacterial infection (which causes problems at a level we can't see), and usually this makes us feel better.

It's the same with believing the events and miracles of the Bible. We weren't there, but we can believe what is recorded there—including the miracles—based on the sober-minded reports of trustworthy people who saw it and wrote it down (along with corroborating evidence of secular history, archaeology, etc.).

It's interesting that Thomas had a similar "I'll believe it when I see it" response to the news of Jesus' resurrection.

The other disciples told [Thomas], "We have seen the Lord!"

But he said to them, "Unless I see the nail marks in his hands and put my finger where the nails were, and put my hand into his side, I will not believe."

A week later his disciples were in the house again, and Thomas was with them. Though the doors were locked, Jesus came and stood among them and said, "Peace be with you!" Then he said to Thomas, "Put your finger here; see my hands. Reach out your hand and put it into my side. Stop doubting and believe."

Thomas said to him, "My Lord and my God!" (John 20:25–28)

And how did Jesus respond to Thomas? He said: "Because you have seen me, you have believed; blessed are those who have not seen and yet have believed" (v. 29). In other words, having direct experience is great, but most of the world will need to rely on the credible testimonies and evidence provided by those who were there—and we're blessed when we do so.

44

What would you say
is the most spectacular
miracle you know of?

Without a doubt, the initial creation of the universe was the most extraordinary miracle ever performed.

"In the beginning there was an explosion," explained Nobel Prize–winning physicist Steven Weinberg. "Not an explosion like those familiar on earth, starting from a definite center and spreading out to engulf more and more of the circumambient air, but an explosion which occurred simultaneously everywhere, filling all space from the beginning, with every particle of matter rushing apart from every other particle."[1]

Within the tiniest split second, the temperature hit a hundred thousand million degrees centigrade. "This is much hotter than in the center of even the hottest star," he wrote.[2]

From an infinitesimal point—which scientists call a *singularity*—the entire universe and time itself exploded into being. The popular theoretical physicist Stephen Hawking added these jaw-dropping details about the unfathomable rate of expansion of the universe resulting immediately from the big bang, or what physicists refer to as "inflation":

> According to even conservative estimates, during this cosmological inflation, the universe expanded by a factor of 1,000,000,000, 000,000,000,000,000,000,000 in .0000000 0000000000000000000000001 second. It was as if a coin 1 centimeter in diameter suddenly blew up to ten million times the width of the Milky Way.[3]

I like the way Mark Mittelberg summarized it:

> This is a highly regarded scientist telling us what virtually every modern scientist believes:

that the universe expanded at a rate equivalent to a coin in your pocket becoming many millions of times wider than our entire galaxy—which all of the efforts of modern space exploration have barely even begun to explore—and it did this in a fraction of a nanosecond! But neither Hawking nor any physicist on earth has a scientific explanation for why or how that happened. In theological terms, we call this a *miracle*.[4]

Yet the very first verse in the Bible explains: "In the beginning God created the heavens and the earth" (Genesis 1:1). As theologians have classically put it, "God created everything *ex nihilo*"—meaning "out of nothing."

It's no wonder the Bible tells us:

> The heavens declare the glory of God;
>> the skies proclaim the work of his
>> hands.
> Day after day they pour forth speech;
>> night after night they reveal
>> knowledge.

They have no speech, they use no words;
   no sound is heard from them.
Yet their voice goes out into all the earth,
   their words to the ends of the
   world. (Psalm 19:1–4)

45

Doesn't the idea of the "big bang" remove the need for a divine Creator?

Not at all. In fact, I think the opposite is true. Let me explain this by presenting an argument from William Lane Craig, a preeminent philosopher and a strong defender of the Christian faith. He helped develop and communicate around the world what he calls the Kalam Cosmological Argument.

Here it is, summarized in three parts:

- Whatever begins to exist has a cause.
- The universe began to exist.
- Therefore, the universe has a cause.[1]

This argument is "extremely strong," said University of Oklahoma physics professor Richard

Strauss. "Think about it: Is there anything that comes into existence without a cause behind it? Some scientists say there may be uncaused quantum events, but I think there are good reasons to be skeptical about that. And we know from the evidence that the universe did come into existence. If those two premises are true, then the conclusion inexorably follows: the universe has a cause."

Given that scientists almost universally believe that the entire physical universe, along with time itself, came into being at the big bang, what can we deduce about the cause behind the universe from the scientific evidence alone?

"Several things," Dr. Strauss told me, grabbing a finger as he mentioned each point. "First, he must be transcendent, because he exists apart from his creation. Second, he must be immaterial or spirit, since he existed before the physical world. Third, he must be timeless or eternal, since he existed before physical time was created. Fourth, he must be powerful, given the immense energy of the big bang. Fifth, he must be smart, given the fact that the big bang was not some chaotic event but was masterfully finely tuned. Sixth, he must be personal, because a decision had to be made to create. Seventh, he must be creative—I mean, just look at the wonders of the universe. And eighth, he must be caring, because he so purposefully crafted a habitat for us."

I don't know about you, but to me that sounds a lot like the Creator I read about in the Bible.

Nobel Prize winner Arno Penzias said this about the big bang: "The best data we have are exactly what I would have predicted had I nothing to go on but the first five books of Moses, the Psalms and the Bible as a whole."[2]

46

What do you think is the most convincing miracle for skeptics?

The famed atheist and author of *God Is Not Great*, Christopher Hitchens, once said, "At some point, certainly, we are all asked which is the best argument you come up against from the other side? I think every one of us picks the fine-tuning one as the most intriguing."[1] Hitchens certainly didn't call this a miracle, but he acknowledged that the strongest evidence we have is the fact that the universe appears to be designed to support life.

"Over the last five decades," said professor Richard Strauss, "physicists have discovered that the numbers which govern the operation of the universe are calibrated with mind-boggling precision so intelligent life can exist. And when I say mind-boggling, I'm not exaggerating. Picture a control board with a hundred different dials and knobs, each representing a different parameter of physics. If you turn any of them just slightly to the left or right—*poof!* Intelligent life becomes impossible anywhere in the universe.

"Even just mistakenly bumping into one of those dials could make the world sterile and barren—or even nonexistent. And that's not only the opinion of Christian scientists. Virtually every scientist agrees the universe is finely tuned—the question is, how did it get this way? I think the most plausible explanation is that the universe was designed by a Creator."

I asked Dr. Strauss for an example of fine-tuning.

"Sure," he answered. "One parameter is the amount of matter in the universe. As the universe expands, all matter is attracted to other matter by gravity. If there were too much matter, the universe would collapse on itself before stars and planets could form. If there were too little matter, stars and planets could never coalesce."

"How finely tuned is the amount of matter?" I asked.

"It turns out that shortly after the big bang, the amount of matter in the universe was precisely tuned to one part in a trillion trillion trillion trillion trillion," he replied. "That's a ten with sixty zeroes after it! In other words, throw in a dime's worth of extra matter and the universe wouldn't exist."

There are so many other examples he could have given, each one independent of the other, and every one tuned to a razor's edge of precision. For me, this scientific data only increases my wonder when I read:

> For in him all things were created: things in heaven and on earth, visible and invisible, whether thrones or powers or rulers or authorities; all things have been created through him and for him. He is before all things, and in him all things hold together. (Colossians 1:16–17)

47

How has the scientific world responded to the evidence for fine-tuning?

While it's not possible to speak for the "scientific world" as a whole, the extraordinary cosmic "coincidences" we've discussed have not escaped secular scientists.

"There is, for me, powerful evidence that there is something going on behind it all," said Paul Davies, a professor of physics at Arizona State University who is an agnostic. "It seems as though somebody has fine-tuned nature's numbers to make the universe. The impression of design is overwhelming."[1]

British cosmologist Edward R. Harrison draws even stronger conclusions from the universe's ultraprecise calibration. "Here is the cosmological proof of the existence of God," he said. "The fine-tuning of the universe provides *prima facie* evidence of deistic design."[2]

British astronomer Sir Fred Hoyle, who claimed to be an atheist, said, "A commonsense interpretation of the facts suggests that a super-intellect has monkeyed with physics, as well as chemistry and biology, and that there are no blind forces worth speaking about in nature. The numbers one calculates from the facts seem to me so overwhelming as to put this conclusion almost beyond question."[3]

And Antony Flew, once considered the world's leading philosophical atheist, after teaching for fifty years at Oxford, Aberdeen, and other world-class universities and writing more than a dozen books attacking the existence of God—including *The Presumption of Atheism*—declared in 2004 that he had been wrong. He said he had begun to believe in a supernatural Creator.

When I had the opportunity to sit down with the aging Dr. Flew, I found him to be thoroughly likable and engaging. Even at eighty-three, he had a sharp mind. When I asked him what evidence caused such a massive shift to his belief in God, he explained, "Einstein felt that there must be intelligence behind the integrated complexity of the physical world. If that is a sound argument, the integrated complexity of the organic world is just inordinately greater—all creatures are complicated pieces of design. So an argument that is important about the physical world is immeasurably stronger when applied to the biological world."

Flew is just one of many skeptics who have felt compelled by scientific discoveries over the last sixty years to conclude that God exists.

"I had to go wherever the evidence took me," he told me. Even if it was to a conclusion that led him to repudiate a lifetime of atheistic scholarship.

48

Why should life on earth be viewed as evidence for the supernatural when so many other planets can sustain life?

Life found anywhere would be evidence for a life-creating being who brought it into existence. But be careful about assuming that "so many other planets can sustain life."

"Our planet," said physics expert Richard Strauss, "is remarkably and fortuitously situated so life would be possible."

"In what way?" I asked.

"To have a planet like ours where life exists, first you need to be in the right kind of galaxy. There are three types of galaxies: elliptical, spiral, and irregular. You need to be in a spiral galaxy, like we are, because it's the only kind that produces the right heavy elements and has the right radiation levels.

"But you can't live just anywhere in the galaxy," he continued. "You have to live in the so-called 'Goldilocks Zone,' or the galactic habitable zone, where life could exist."

Strauss continued: "To have life, you need a star like our sun. Our sun is a Class G star that has supported stable planet orbits in the right location for a long time. The star must be in its middle age, so its luminosity is stabilized. It has to be a bachelor star. . . . Plus, the star should be a third-generation star, like our sun."

Strauss was on a roll. "There are so many parameters that have to be just right for our planet to support life," he said. "The distance from the sun, the rotation rate, the amount of water, the tilt, the right size so gravity lets gases like methane escape but allows oxygen to stay. You need a moon like ours—it's very rare to have just one large moon—in order to stabilize the earth's tilt. As counterintuitive as it sounds, you even need to have tectonic activity, which experts said could be 'the central requirement for life on a planet.'"[1]

"How many conditions have to be met to create an Earth-like planet?" I asked.

"Hugh Ross sets the number at three hundred and twenty-two,"[2] he replied, referring to the noted astrophysicist. "So if you run probability calculations, you find that there's a 10^{-304} chance you're going to find another planet that's truly like earth."

"Still, there are lots of potential candidates out there," I pointed out. "One estimate is there could be more than a billion trillion planets."

"Granted," he said. "So let's factor that number into our probability equation. That still means the odds of having any higher life-supporting planet would be one in a million trillion.

"In science, we have a phrase for probabilities like that: *'Ain't gonna happen.'*"

49

What if there is an infinite number of universes, and we're just fortunate to be in one that sustains life?

You're referring to the so-called *multiverse* hypothesis. Here's the argument: "There could have been millions and millions of different universes each created with different dial settings of the fundamental ratios and constants, so many in fact that the right set was bound to turn up by sheer chance. We just happened to be the lucky ones."[1]

Put another way, if ours is the only universe, then the fine-tuning is powerful evidence for an intelligence behind it. That seems obvious unless, as proponents of the multiverse would say, there are an infinite number of universes. With enough random dial spinning, the odds are that at least one universe—ours—would win the cosmic lottery and be a livable habitat.

What are we to make of this claim?

"It's purely a concept, an idea, without scientific proof," said William Lane Craig, coauthor of *Theism, Atheism, and Big Bang Cosmology.* "Look—this is pure metaphysics. There's no real reason to believe such parallel worlds exist. The very fact that skeptics have to come up with such an outlandish theory is because the fine-tuning of the universe points powerfully toward an Intelligent Designer—and some people will hypothesize anything to avoid reaching that conclusion."[2]

Professor Richard Strauss adds, "Physicists have come up with various ideas for how multiverses could be birthed, but again, there's no observational or experimental evidence for it. In fact, there is likely no way for us to discover something that's beyond our universe. And even if there were multiple universes . . . they all must go back to one beginning point, so now we return to the question of who or what created the universe in the first place."

His conclusion? "If you want to believe in one of the multiverse theories, you basically need blind faith."

John Polkinghorne, former professor of mathematical physics at Cambridge, said: "The many universes account is sometimes presented as if it were purely scientific, but in fact a sufficient portfolio of different universes could only be generated by speculative processes that go well beyond what sober science can honestly endorse."[3]

Richard Swinburne of Oxford was even more to-the-point: "To postulate a trillion-trillion other universes, rather than one God, in order to explain the orderliness of our universe, seems the height of irrationality."[4]

Me? I don't have enough faith to believe in an infinite number of uncreated, purposeless universes—for which there is no evidence—somehow resulting in one like ours, full of intelligence and purpose.

50

What do you think is the most important miracle God ever performed?

I said earlier that the creation of the universe was God's most spectacular miracle—but assuming you're asking what God's most important miracle was *after* creation, then I would say it's clearly the resurrection of Jesus.

Why? Because it's the make-or-break event of our faith and future. Jesus himself staked his claims on his coming resurrection. You might remember that the religious leaders were pressing him for a miraculous sign in order to prove who he was. He answered them by saying, "None will be given it except the sign of the prophet Jonah. For as Jonah was three days and three nights in the belly of a huge fish, so the Son of Man will be three days and three nights in the heart of the earth" (Matthew 12:39–40). In other words, Jesus predicted that after his coming execution, he would be in the grave only three days before rising from the dead—and that would be the proof they were looking for.

Paul underscored this when he explained in 1 Corinthians 15:17–19, "If Christ has not been raised, your faith is futile; you are still in your sins. Then those also who have fallen asleep in Christ are lost. If only for this life we have hope in Christ, we are of all people most to be pitied."

Even when I was a skeptic investigating the claims of Christ, I immediately recognized that the resurrection is the linchpin of the Christian faith. It is the supreme vindication of Jesus' divine identity and inspired teaching. It's the proof of his triumph over sin and death. It's the foreshadowing of the resurrection of his followers. It's the basis of all Christian hope.

That's why I investigated the evidence for it so carefully. Eventually, by God's grace, I found the facts I needed, and they pointed to several essential truths of the Christian worldview. These are summed up in Romans 10:9–10:

> If you declare with your mouth, "Jesus is Lord," and believe in your heart that God raised him from the dead, you will be saved. For it is with your heart that you believe and are justified, and it is with your mouth that you profess your faith and are saved.

There are three nonnegotiable truths in this passage that a person must believe in order to receive salvation. First, that "Jesus is Lord"—which points to his divine nature as the Son of God. Second, that Jesus died for our sins. And third, that "God raised him from the dead." According to this passage, we must genuinely embrace these three truths in order to receive salvation. I did just that, and for me it changed *everything*.

51

What was the evidence that convinced you Jesus really rose from the dead?

That's a big question to answer in such a small space! Entire books have been written about this, including much of what's in my books *The Case for Christ*, *In Defense of Jesus*, and *The Case for Miracles*. That said, let me summarize some of the main points I found persuasive, using six words that start with the letter *E*:[1]

1. *Execution—Jesus really died on the cross.*

    Jesus didn't pass out on the cross or fake his death. These were once common theories among skeptics, but they've been thoroughly discredited. The evidence shows that Jesus died even before the spear was thrust into his side to doubly ensure his demise.

2. *Empty Tomb—Jesus' body was missing.*

On that first Easter morning, women discovered that Jesus' body was gone. Peter and John soon confirmed the empty tomb for themselves. Even Jesus' enemies implicitly admitted this by making up stories to explain why his body was missing.

3. *Eyewitnesses—The risen Jesus appeared to many.*

The disciples saw the risen Savior for themselves—some of them multiple times. Over forty days Jesus appeared to both individuals and groups in a variety of places and circumstances. We have nine ancient sources, inside and outside the New Testament, confirming the conviction of the disciples that they had encountered the risen Christ.[2]

4. *Early Accounts—These facts were reported early and often.*

Multiple reports of Jesus' resurrection were circulating during the lifetimes of

Jesus' contemporaries—people who would have been all too happy to point out the errors if the accounts had not been true. In fact, the earliest report of Jesus' rising comes in a creed that was formulated within months of his resurrection (1 Corinthians 15:3–7).

5. *Extrabiblical Reports—There's strong confirmation outside the Bible.*

Secular accounts confirm the contours of the New Testament record. Thirty-nine ancient sources provide more than one hundred facts about Jesus' life, teachings, death, and resurrection.[3]

6. *Emergence of the Church—Its birth in Jerusalem supports its claims.*

Apart from the resurrection, it's hard to explain the beginnings of the church, which emerged in the very city where Jesus had been crucified a few weeks earlier. The church grew out of the claim that he had come back to life. If false, it easily could have been disproven.

"God has raised this Jesus to life," said Peter, "and we are all witnesses of it" (Acts 2:32). After almost two years of studying the evidence for the resurrection, I had to agree.

52

Much of the evidence for the resurrection is based on eyewitnesses. But aren't they often unreliable?

I asked that question of J. Warner Wallace, a renowned detective, author of *Cold-Case Christianity,* and, like me, a skeptic-turned-Christian.

"No question—all eyewitness accounts have to be tested for reliability. In California, judges give jurors more than a dozen factors to weigh in evaluating an eyewitness account," he said. "We can apply these tests to the Gospels—for instance, is there any corroboration, did the witnesses have a motive to lie, did their stories change over time? When we do, we find they hold up well."

"How early do you date the Gospels?"

"Acts doesn't report several major events that occurred during the AD 60s—including the martyrdoms of Paul, Peter, and James—apparently because it was written before they occurred. We know Luke's Gospel came before Acts, and we know Mark was written before Luke, because he uses it as one of his sources. Even before that, Paul confirms the resurrection in material that goes back to within a few years of Jesus' execution.[1] When you consider Jesus died in AD 30 or 33, the gap shrinks to where it's not a problem."

"So it doesn't bother you that the Gospels were passed along verbally before being written down?" I asked.

"Not at all. I've seen witnesses in cold cases say their memories from thirty-five years ago are like it happened yesterday. Why? Because not all memories are created the same."

"What do you mean?"

"If you asked me what I did on Valentine's Day five years ago, I probably couldn't recall very much. That's because it's only one of many Valentine's Days I've celebrated with Susie. But if you asked me about Valentine's Day of 1988, I can give you a detailed report of what took place."

"Why's that?"

"Because that's the day Susie and I got married," he replied. "When witnesses experience something that's unique, unrepeated, and personally important or powerful, they're much more likely to remember it. Of course, many of the disciples' experiences with Jesus met those criteria.

"Can they remember all the times their boat got stuck in a storm?" he asked. "Probably not, but they could remember the time Jesus quieted the squall. And think of the resurrection—as much as anything they experienced, that was unique, unrepeated, and extremely powerful."

As Wallace said, eyewitnesses need to be tested. But once they pass the test, they are one of our best sources of reliable information.

53

What about the discrepancies between the Gospels? Do they discredit the miracle of the resurrection?

B ased on my years as a detective, I would *expect* the four Gospels to have variances," detective J. Warner Wallace told me. "Think of this: the early believers could have destroyed all but one of the Gospels in order to eliminate any differences between them. But they didn't. Why? Because they knew the Gospels were true and that they told the story from different perspectives, emphasizing different things."

"The conflicts aren't evidence they were lying?" I asked.

"People might assume that if they've never worked with eyewitnesses before. In my experience, eyewitness accounts can be reliable despite discrepancies. Besides, if they meshed too perfectly, it would be evidence of collusion."

That reminded me of something written by Simon Greenleaf of Harvard Law School, one of America's key legal scholars, after he had studied the Gospels. "There is enough of a discrepancy to show that there could have been no previous concert among them," he declared, "and at the same time such substantial agreement as to show that they all were independent narrators of the same great transaction."[1]

"What's your conclusion?" I asked Wallace.

"The most reasonable explanation is that the Gospels were penned by different eyewitnesses who were just reporting what they saw," he replied.

"So this was one more piece to the puzzle for you," I said.

"One of many. We have archaeology corroborating certain points of the Gospels. We have non-Christian accounts outside the Bible that provide confirmation of key gospel claims. We have students of the apostles who give a consistent account of what the disciples were teaching. And we have a proliferation of ancient manuscripts that help us get back to what the original Gospels said."

"Okay then, Mr. Detective. What's your verdict?"

"That the Gospels can be messy, that they're filled with idiosyncrasies, that they're each told from a different perspective and have variances between them—just like you'd expect from a collection of eyewitness accounts," he said. "So I became convinced that they constitute reliable testimony to the life, teachings, death, and—yes, the resurrection—of Jesus."

I wholeheartedly concur. For these reasons, and many others, I believe that history shows Jesus did what he said he'd do. He died on the cross to pay for our sins, and he rose again three days later to give us new life.

54

What kind of impact does the miracle of Jesus' resurrection have on individual lives?

The resurrection of Jesus is a cosmic event with a personal impact," said my friends Kerry and Chris Shook in their book *Find Your Miracle*.[1] That was true back then, in the lives of Jesus' immediate friends and followers—as well as those who were skeptical, like James and Paul. The appearance of the risen Savior had a way of stopping people in their tracks and instantly turning their lives around.

That's true today as well. I've already described how the facts supporting the resurrection compelled me to acknowledge Jesus as the Son of God who came to save me from my sins. The day I finally owned up to that reality, my life was turned around.

The examples are endless. There's J. Warner Wallace, the cold-case detective who decided to tackle the oldest case he'd ever encountered—one that was two thousand years old. In the process he subjected the Gospels to months of painstaking analysis through various investigative techniques, including what detectives call "forensic statement analysis," before finally realizing that he could trust the biblical record—including the reports of Jesus' rising from the dead. Ultimately Wallace put his trust in him and today, he told me, "my life is consumed by letting others know that faith in Christ isn't just a subjective emotion, but it's grounded in the truth of the resurrection."

I also think of Jewish friends who researched the information for themselves and eventually trusted in Christ. There's Louis Lapides, who was prodded by a street evangelist, went on a quest to find Jesus in the Jewish scriptures, and through the ancient prophecies realized that Jesus fulfilled the predictions of the Messiah against all odds.[2]

And the late Stan Telchin, a spirited insurance broker who set out to expose the "cult" of

Christianity after his daughter went away to college and received *Y'shua* (Jesus) as her Messiah. His investigation led him to the resurrected Jesus, and he later became a pastor. He tells the story in his autobiographical book, *Betrayed!* which has impacted the lives of countless other Jewish people.[3]

As with Wallace, the miracle of the resurrection led these Jewish friends to a spiritual transformation that was extraordinary. They exchanged their sin for God's grace, experienced a profound spiritual rebirth, and were changed in ways that were simply inexplicable in ordinary human terms.

That's the enduring power of the miracle of Jesus' resurrection.

55

You've written that many Christians are "embarrassed by the supernatural." Can you explain?

I read a blog in which theology professor Roger Olson asserted that many churches and individual Christians seem embarrassed by miracles. When I met with him and asked him for one word to summarize why he thinks this is the case, he replied, "Respectability."

"Why that word?" I asked.

"Evangelicals in general are trying to live down our past," he replied. "We're very aware of Hollywood's version of us—the oddball preacher, the phony faith healer, the hyperemotional revivalist, the money-grubbing hypocrite. We want to run from those depictions. We want our neighbors to see us as normal people who are not very different from them. We are desperate to fit in."

"So," I said, "we divorce ourselves from the supernatural, since it seems odd to the world."

"That's right. We want to show that we're cultured and refined, that we're not gullible or superstitious, that we're not like the over-the-top fanatics that our neighbors see on television. In fact," he added, "my experience is that the richer and more educated evangelicals become, the less likely they are to really expect miracles to happen."

"Why is that? Too sophisticated?"

"I could almost predict by the brand of cars in the parking lot what the church believes. The more prosperous and educated we are, the more likely we are to substitute our own cleverness and accomplishments for the power of prayer. That's the seductive power of prosperity—it makes us less reliant on God. We think we've got everything under control."

This squares with the Bible's warning in Deuteronomy 8:10–11: "When you have eaten and are satisfied, praise the LORD your God for the good land he has given you. Be careful that you do not forget the LORD your God."

Olson added a thought that I could identify with: "Many evangelicals don't really believe in the supernatural until the doctor says, 'You have a terminal illness.'"

I remember lying in a hospital bed several years ago, where I was told that I could be facing death. I suddenly felt desperately vulnerable and much more dependent on God to rescue me. No question about it—times like that strip away our self-sufficiency and leave us frantic for God's direct supernatural touch.

Thankfully, God came through for me in that situation, but the key—for me and for you—is to resolve to stay close to him and expectant of his supernatural activity in our lives, with or without a crisis experience.

56

How does our experience
of God's supernatural
activities in the West
compare to other places?

Roger Olson's classes at Baylor University
attract students from all around the world,
including developing countries where Christianity
and its experience of the supernatural look very
different from what it tends to look like here in
the West.

"When these African and Asian students
see Western evangelicalism for the first time,
what's their assessment?" I asked the professor of
theology.

"They have to be coaxed to give it," Olson said.
"But when they do, it's total dismay."

"How so?" I asked.

"They say, 'This is not our Christianity. Our Christianity in Africa is surrounded by spiritual warfare. We can't brush it off as superstition. God really intervenes and does amazing things, but we don't see that here. We think it's your prosperity, individualism, materialism, and a lack of belief in the spiritual world,' by which they mean the supernatural."

Olson told me about the time he invited a Catholic priest from Nigeria to address his class. "He didn't want to talk about Catholic doctrine," Olson said. "He wanted to talk about miracles. For an hour and twenty minutes, he talked about God's supernatural actions in Nigeria."

"How did the students react?"

"They were in awe," he said. "They couldn't believe it."

"Did it light a fire in the students?"

"For sure."

"Some people say the reason miracles proliferate in Africa and other places in the Third World is because that's the leading edge of the gospel," I said.

"Yes, Benjamin Warfield first made that argument in a book called *Counterfeit Miracles* in the early twentieth century," he replied.

"What do you think of that claim?"

Olson's reply was strong and direct. "It's nonsense."

"Really?" I replied.

"We need the supernatural as much as they do in China. America is still a mission field. I suspect that real Christianity is a minority even among people who call themselves Christian. Too often we think we only need apologetics, evidence, debates, and arguments to spread the gospel here, rather than to see God do a supernatural work."

Olson makes a good point. I think we need all of the above—including a lot more of God's supernatural work, spiritually turbocharging our ministry efforts and opening more and more hearts to him.

57

How can I handle the disappointment of not having my prayers answered . . . of not getting a miracle?

That's the question I asked Christian philosopher and author Douglas Groothuis, whose wife Becky suffered from primary progressive aphasia—a debilitating, incurable, and invariably fatal brain disease—before she finally passed away on July 6, 2018.

"I've learned to lament," Groothuis said. "Sixty of the psalms are laments. There's lament in Ecclesiastes and Job. Jesus laments over the unbelief of Jerusalem. On the cross, his lament came as the cry, 'My God, my God, why have you forsaken me?'[1] If Jesus can lament and not sin, then I suppose *we* can. And just as his lament was answered by his resurrection, so ours will be too.

"Look—God's good world has been broken by sin, and it's morally and spiritually right to lament the loss of a true good. I'm grateful for the lament we see in Scripture—it's God helping us learn how to suffer well."

"Suffer well?" I echoed. "Sounds oxymoronic."

"That phrase can take people aback. They say, 'Suffering can't be done well; it's bad.' No, you can suffer well when you admit your grief, when you pray despite not feeling like you want to, when you're honest with God, and when you don't paper over your emotions."

"That's messy, no doubt," I said.

"Very. And I haven't always suffered well. I've gone over the line at times. I've told God that I hated him for what was happening. That was a heartfelt expression of my grief at the time, but I don't want to impugn God. He too bears scars— the scars of your sins and mine. Jesus suffered far more than you or I ever will."

"Even Martin Luther supposedly said, 'Love God? Sometimes I hate him!'" I said. "How do you get beyond those emotions?"

"In the end, I know too much to think that God isn't perfectly good," he replied. "I'm grateful he allows us to vent our frustration. Read Ecclesiastes or the psalms of lament—they are startlingly honest. For me, I found that there's a practice that helps put everything into perspective."

"What's that?"

"When I'm angry at God, when I'm distressed and anguished and seething at my circumstances, I think of Christ hanging on the cross for me. This brings me back to spiritual sanity. He endured the torture of the crucifixion out of his love for me. He didn't have to do that. He chose to. So he doesn't just sympathize with us in our suffering; he empathizes with us. Ultimately, I find comfort in that."

And so do I.

58

When miracles don't happen
and suffering continues,
which worldview offers
the best answers?

A theism doesn't give a sufficient answer,"
Professor Douglas Groothuis reminded me.
"Under that philosophy, the world is meaningless
and there's no purpose for life. Islam believes in a
personal God, but not in a savior. Pantheism doesn't
have a God who cares about the plight of people.

"Compare Jesus with Buddha. The first of the
four noble truths of Buddhism is suffering. It's not
that there is suffering in a good world, but life *is*
suffering. The Buddha's answer is to escape the
world and enter nirvana through a change of consciousness—to depersonalize yourself and sort of
float out of the world. There's no resurrection, no
redemption, no savior.

"Christianity is so different," Groothuis continued. "Think of Jesus at the tomb of Lazarus. Jesus weeps; he identifies with the suffering of Lazarus's sisters. They're angry—'Why, Jesus, didn't you come earlier? You could have healed him and he wouldn't have died.' That's pretty impious, but what does Jesus do? He restores Lazarus to life.[1] For us, the message is clear: there is a future, there is hope, there is resurrection, there will be a new body in a world without tears."

"Still," I said, "evil is a challenge for Christianity too, because God is all-good and all-powerful, and yet there's so much suffering."

"Christianity has the best explanation for evil and suffering because of the fall of humanity. Ever since then, the world has been plagued by death, decay, and disappointment. But because Christ experienced the worst of the world and triumphed over it and is now at the right hand of the Father, then I know there will be a resurrection, and my wife and I will live in the new heaven and the new earth. Granted, God has not dealt with suffering and evil completely, but we have the assurance that he will. You see, there's a difference between meaningless suffering and inscrutable suffering."

"What's that?" I asked.

"*Meaningless suffering* means that suffering is simply there; it doesn't achieve a greater good, it has no purpose. *Inscrutable suffering* means we don't know what the purpose is, but we have reason to believe that God is providential, loving, and all-powerful. Our suffering may seem meaningless to us, but it's not. Here's the point: God uses evil to produce a greater good that could not be achieved otherwise—though we may not understand how, given our finite intelligence and our fallible nature."

I appreciated Groothuis's insights, which made a lot more sense than anything I've seen from alternative worldviews. They were also reminiscent of Jesus in John 16:33: "I have told you these things, so that in me you may have peace. In this world you will have trouble. But take heart! I have overcome the world."

59

Do you have any thoughts
for those who still doubt the
possibility of miracles?

My main advice would be to try to examine what's holding you back—is it really a
lack of *evidence*, or might it be a lack of *openness*?
The Bible says we tend to suppress the truth and
intentionally turn our backs on God. I've seen that
play out in my own life. Years ago I didn't want
Christianity to be true. I was living a self-centered
life—and wanted to keep it that way.

But then my wife, Leslie, committed her life
to Christ. She immediately began to change for
the better. I was sometimes drawn to that, but
more often I just wanted the old Leslie back. So I
came up with a plan to try to make that happen.
I reasoned that if I could disprove Jesus' resurrection, then I'd not only debunk Christianity but

also have strong grounds for pulling Leslie out of the church.

As I embarked on my investigation, I realized I would be wasting my time if I began with a foregone conclusion. From my journalism training I knew I needed to keep an open mind and to do my best to set aside my biases as I pursued answers.

I immediately discovered something that surprised me: Christianity *invites* investigation. In fact, the apostle Paul said if you can show that the miracle of the resurrection didn't happen, then you'd be justified in walking away from the faith. I also noticed that accounts of miracles never begin with "Once upon a time." Rather they're written in a serious tone, often with details that can be checked out concerning the who, what, where, when, and why of the things being reported.

After almost two years of research, I reached my verdict concerning the Christian story, including the claims, miracles, and resurrection of Jesus who—I now believed—showed himself to be the unique Son of God. The evidence for all of this was strong, adding up to a cumulative case for Christ

that I found to be compelling. So, propelled by what I had learned, I finally joined Leslie in following Jesus. If you'd known me back then, I think you'd conclude that had to be a *miracle!*

I share all of this to explain that the more I looked into the evidence, the greater my confidence in a miracle-working God became. And I think the same will be true for you or anyone who doubts, but who is willing to investigate with an open heart and mind.

Jesus said in Matthew 7:7, "Seek and you will find."

60

You've convinced me
miracles really do happen.
But what difference should
that make in my life?

Let me mention again what we said at the beginning: a genuine miracle is not just an unusual
or seemingly supernatural occurrence. Rather, it
is *an event brought about by the power of God that
is a temporary exception to the ordinary course of
nature for the purpose of showing that God has
acted in history.*[1]

Why is it important to know God acted in history? It's so we'll know he is able to continue to
work today—in our world and in our lives.

That's why I'm a theist, not a deist. I don't
believe God wound up the world in the distant
past and then walked away, leaving us to fend for
ourselves. No, he is present and active, revealing

himself not only through inspired words but also through miraculous works.

Specifically, the miracle of *creation* tells us he is a powerful and wise God who cares a lot about us. The miracle of *the incarnation of Christ* tells us God loves us enough to come and die in our place. The miracle of *the resurrection* tells us Jesus really is who he claimed to be—the divine Son of God—and that he is alive again and able to give us new life. The miracle of *salvation* tells us when we put our faith in Christ our sins are truly forgiven, and we can know that we have eternal life with him. And *all of the other miracles* tell us that God is able to help us with our every challenge.

So our response to miracles should be to ask God what else he wants to do in us. "The deeper miracle He wants to do in your life," Kerry and Chris Shook explain, "is to draw you closer to Himself so you'll discover the whole reason He created you. And that is to be in a deep and lasting love relationship with the Source of all miracles."[2]

Each of us needs "the miracle of salvation—God rescuing us, pulling us out of our sin, redeeming us. This is the work of Jesus taking on our sins so the veil can be torn away and God can be present with us, not distant and separate. This is the miracle of eternal life with God, life that starts now and continues beyond time."[3]

This is the most important miracle we can ever experience—because through it we come to know God himself. So reach out to him today; admit your sins and receive his salvation. Then go share him and his mighty works with others who need to know him as you do.

Recommended Resources

Kevin Belmonte, *Miraculous: A Fascinating History of Signs, Wonders, and Miracles* (Nashville: Thomas Nelson, 2012).

Craig S. Keener, *Miracles: The Credibility of the New Testament Accounts,* 2 volumes (Grand Rapids: Baker Academic, 2011).

C. S. Lewis, *Miracles: A Preliminary Study* (New York: HarperOne, 2001).

Eric Metaxas, *Miracles: What They Are, Why They Happen, and How They Can Change Your Life* (New York: Dutton, 2014).

Tim Stafford, *Miracles: A Journalist Looks at Modern-Day Experiences of God's Power* (Minneapolis: Bethany House, 2012).

Lee Strobel, *The Case for Miracles: A Journalist Investigates Evidence for the Supernatural* (Grand Rapids: Zondervan, 2018).

Lee Strobel, *The Case for a Creator: Scientific Evidence That Points Toward God* (Grand Rapids: Zondervan, 2004).

Lee Strobel, *The Case for Christ: A Journalist's Personal Investigation of the Evidence for Jesus* (Grand Rapids: Zondervan, 1998; Updated and Expanded Edition, 2016). Also available as a feature film on DVD and Blu-ray (Pure Flix, 2017).

About the Authors

Lee Strobel

Atheist-turned-Christian Lee Strobel, the award-winning legal editor of the *Chicago Tribune*, is a *New York Times* bestselling author of more than twenty books. He formerly taught First Amendment law at Roosevelt University.

Lee was educated at the University of Missouri (Bachelor of Journalism degree) and Yale Law School (Master of Studies in Law degree). He was a journalist for fourteen years at the *Chicago Tribune* and other newspapers, winning the highest honor in Illinois for public service journalism from United Press International. He also led a team that won UPI's top award for investigative reporting in Illinois.

After examining the evidence for Jesus, Lee became a Christian in 1981. He subsequently became a teaching pastor at two of America's most influential churches and hosted the national network TV program *Faith Under Fire*. Now he is a teaching pastor at Woodlands Church in Texas.

Lee has won national awards for his books *The Case for Christ*, *The Case for Faith*, *The Case for a Creator*, and *The Case for Grace*. In 2017, his spiritual journey was depicted in a major motion picture, *The Case for Christ*, which ranks among the top twenty faith-based films at the box office.

Lee and his wife, Leslie, have been married for over forty-five years. Their daughter, Alison, is a novelist. Their son, Kyle, is a professor of spiritual theology at the Talbot School of Theology at Biola University.

Mark Mittelberg

Mark Mittelberg is a bestselling author, sought-after speaker, and leading outreach strategist.

Mark is the primary author of the celebrated *Becoming a Contagious Christian* training course (coauthored with Lee Strobel). This course has been translated into more than twenty languages and has trained more than 1.5 million people around the world to share Christ in natural and effective ways.

Mark wrote *Confident Faith*—winner of *Outreach* magazine's 2014 apologetics book of the year—and *The Reason Why: Faith Makes Sense*, an update of a classic that has touched millions of lives. He authored *The Questions Christians Hope No One Will Ask (With Answers)*, and he collaborated with Strobel to write *The Unexpected Adventure* as well as the *Making Your Case for Christ* video curriculum and the apologetics devotional, *The Case for Christ Daily Moment of Truth*. Mark's other books include *Becoming a Contagious Church* and

Becoming a Contagious Christian, coauthored with Bill Hybels.

Mark was the original evangelism director at Willow Creek Community Church near Chicago. He later served as executive vice president of the Willow Creek Association. After receiving an undergraduate degree in business management, Mark earned a master's degree in philosophy of religion, graduating magna cum laude from Trinity Evangelical Divinity School. Mark and Heidi live near Denver, Colorado, and have two grown children.

Notes

Introduction

1. Unless otherwise noted, quotations in this volume are taken from my book, Lee Strobel, *The Case for Miracles* (Grand Rapids, MI: Zondervan, 2018).

Chapter 1: What do you mean by *miracle?* I hear that term used in so many ways.

1. For these and many other definitions and their citations, see Michael R. Licona, *The Resurrection of Jesus: A New Historiographical Approach* (Downers Grove, IL: IVP Academic, 2010), 134–136.

2. Richard L. Purtill, "Defining Miracles" in Douglas Geivett and Gary R. Habermas, eds., *In Defense of Miracles* (Downers Grove, IL: InterVarsity, 1997), 72.

Chapter 2: Can you explain the difference between a divine miracle and an ordinary coincidence?

1. Richard L. Purtill, "Defining Miracles" in Douglas Geivett and Gary R. Habermas, eds., *In Defense of Miracles* (Downers Grove, IL: InterVarsity, 1997), 61–62.

Chapter 4: How common are miracles? Aren't they pretty rare?

1. A random, representative study of one thousand US adults completed this questionnaire. The sample error is +/- 3.1 percent points at the 95 percent confidence level. The response rate was 55 percent. The survey conducted as research for this book began in 2015.

2. Based on 2016 US government estimate of the population over the age of eighteen at 249,454,440. See www.census.gov/quickfacts/fact/table/US/.

Chapter 5: Aren't claims of miracles more common among uneducated people?

1. Harriet Hall, "On Miracles," *Skeptic* 19, no. 3 (2014), 18.
2. This survey was conducted by HCD Research and the Louis Finkelstein Institute for Religious and Social Studies of the Jewish Theological Seminary. See "Science or Miracle?; Holiday Season Reveals Physicians' View of Faith, Prayer and Miracles," *BusinessWire,* December 20, 2004, www.businesswire.com/news /home/20041220005244/en/Science-Miracle -Holiday-Season-Survey-Reveals-Physicians.
3. "Science or Miracle?"

Chapter 6: Have you heard stories of dreams that you would consider to be miraculous?

1. Anugrah Kumar, "Ben Carson Says God Helped Him Ace College Chemistry Exam by Giving Answers in Dream," *The Christian Post,* May 9, 2015, www.christianpost.com /news/ben-carson-says-God-helped-him-ace -college-chemistry-exam-by-giving-answers-in -dream-138913.

Chapter 7: You were once a skeptical journalist. What made you start believing in miracles?

1. Nicholas Kristof, "Am I a Christian, Pastor Timothy Keller?" *New York Times*, December 23, 2016.

Chapter 9: Have you ever seen or experienced a divine healing?

1. See www.Nuvoice.org. Also, Duane Miller tells his story in *Speechless* (Houston, TX: Worldwide, 2017) and *Out of the Silence: A Personal Testimony of God's Healing Power* (Nashville, TN: Thomas Nelson, 1996).

Chapter 12: David Hume said miracles would violate the laws of nature, and therefore they are impossible. Your response?

1. See Mark J. Larson, "Three Centuries of Objections to Biblical Miracles," *Bibliotheca Sacra* 160 (2003): 87.
2. David Johnson, *Hume, Holism, and Miracles* (Ithaca, NY: Cornell University Press, 1999), front flap.
3. Johnson, *Hume, Holism, and Miracles*, 4.

Chapter 13: How can we best scrutinize stories about miracles?

1. Jerry A. Coyne, *Faith vs. Fact: Why Science and Religion Are Incompatible* (New York: Viking, 2015), 124.

2. For a response to this contention by physicist Michael G. Strauss, see Michael G. Strauss, "Extraordinary Claims and Extraordinary Evidence," *Dr. Michael G. Strauss* blog, May 21, 2017, www.michaelgstrauss.com/2017/05/extraordinary-claims-and-extraordinary.html.

Chapter 16: Can God still raise people from the dead today?

1. See Chauncey W. Crandall IV, *Raising the Dead* (New York: FaithWords, 2010), 1–5.

Chapter 19: Why doesn't God always answer my prayers and give me what I ask for?

1. Tricia Lott Williford, "When Everyone Else Is Getting Their Miracle: How to Deal with Feeling Overlooked," *Ann Voskamp* blog, July 10, 2017, www.annvoskamp.com/2017/07/when-everyone-else-is-getting-their-miracle-how-to-deal-with-feeling-overlooked.

Chapter 20: Haven't studies proven that prayer doesn't make any difference?

1. H. Benson, J. A. Dusek, et al., "Study of the Therapeutic Effects of Intercessory Prayer (STEP) in Cardiac Bypass Patients: A Multicenter Randomized Trial of Uncertainty and Certainty of Receiving Intercessory Prayer," *American Heart Journal*, April 2006.

2. Quoting May Rowland, Silent Unity's director from 1916 to 1971. See Neal Vahle, *The Unity Movement: Its Evolution and Spiritual Teachings* (Philadelphia, PA: Templeton Foundation Press, 2002), 246–247.

Chapter 25: Aren't there a lot of fake miracles?

1. Harriet Hall, "On Miracles," *Skeptic* 19, no. 3 (2014), 17–23.

Chapter 26: Can a miracle be real but not be from God?

1. These elements are from the definition for biblical miracles from Richard L. Purtill, "Defining Miracles," in: Douglas Geivett and Gary R. Habermas, editors., *In Defense of Miracles* (Downers Grove, IL: InterVarsity, 1997), 72.

Chapter 28: Can God heal a broken heart?
   1. See www.BuildYourMarriage.org, led by Brad and Heidi Mitchell.

Chapter 29: What about a physical heart—can God heal that too?
   1. "I can do all this through him who gives me strength" (Philippians 4:13).
   2. Interestingly, the visiting minister, Wesley Steelberg Jr., had himself been healed of a heart condition after being given just hours to live. See Craig S. Keener, *Miracles: The Credibility of the New Testament Accounts*, 2 vols. (Grand Rapids: Baker Academic, 2011), 432, note 26.

Chapter 30: What would you say to a cessationist—a Christian who doesn't believe miracles still happen today?
   1. John Piper, "Are Signs and Wonders for Today?" *Desiring God* blog, February 25, 1990, www.desiringgod.org/messages /are-signs-and-wonders-for-today.

Chapter 31: Why trust the biblical
accounts of Jesus' miracles? Weren't
the writers biased, since they were
already believers?

1. http://coldcasechristianity.com/2018/is-marks
   -gospel-an-early-memoir-of-the-apostle-peter
   /; https://crossexamined.org/wrote-gospel
   -mark/.

Chapter 32: Does believing in the
evidence for miracles compete
with simple faith in God?

1. A lecture by Richard Dawkins extracted
   from *The Nullifidian* (December 1994, http://
   www.simonyi.ox.ac.uk/dawkins
   /WorldOfDawkins-archive/Dawkins/Work
   /Articles/1994-12religion.shtml.
2. See Nabeel Qureshi, *Seeking Allah, Finding Jesus:
   A Devout Muslim Encounters Christianity* (Grand
   Rapids, MI: Zondervan, 3rd ed., 2018).

Chapter 33: How did your Muslim friend
know that his dreams were from God?

1. Luke 13:22–26, 28–29.

Chapter 34: Why do you think
so many Muslims are having
dreams about Jesus?

1. Lee Strobel, *The Case for Faith* (Grand Rapids,
   MI: Zondervan, 2000), 162.
2. Tom Doyle with Greg Webster, *Dreams and
   Visions* (Nashville, TN: Thomas Nelson, 2012),
   127.

Chapter 36: Is this Muslim dream
phenomenon limited to the
Middle East?

1. Nik Ripken, *The Insanity of God: A True Story
   of Faith Resurrected,* (Nashville, TN: B&H
   Publishing Group, 2013), 280.
2. Ibid., 279.

Chapter 38: Do these dreams really
change people's lives, or are they just
passing curiosities?

1. Nabeel Qureshi, *Seeking Allah, Finding Jesus:
   A Devout Muslim Encounters Christianity*
   (Grand Rapids, MI: Zondervan, 3rd ed.,
   2018), 252–253.

Chapter 42: If God wants more followers, why doesn't he just do more miracles in order to convince everyone?

1. Blaise Pascal, *Pensées,* (430), (New York: E. P. Dutton & Co., Inc., 1958), 118.

Chapter 44: What would you say is the most spectacular miracle you know of?

1. Steven Weinberg, *The First Three Minutes*, updated ed. (New York: Basic Books, 1988), 5.
2. Weinberg, *First Three Minutes*.
3. Stephen Hawking and Leonard Mlodinow, *The Grand Design* (New York: Bantam Books, 2010), 129.
4. Mark Mittelberg, *The Reason Why Faith Makes Sense* (Carol Stream, IL: Tyndale, 2011), 14–15.

Chapter 45: Doesn't the idea of the "big bang" remove the need for a divine Creator?

1. William Lane Craig, *On Guard*: *Defending Your Faith with Reason and Precision* (Colorado Springs, CO: David C. Cook, 2010), 74.
2. See Malcolm W. Browne, "Clues to Universe Origin Expected," *New York Times*, March 12, 1978.

Chapter 46: What do you think is the most convincing miracle for skeptics?

1. "Christopher Hitchens Makes a Shocking Confession," accessed September 1, 2016, www.youtube.com/watch?v=E9TMwfkDwIY.

Chapter 47: How has the scientific world responded to the evidence for fine-tuning?

1. Paul Davies, *The Cosmic Blueprint* (New York: Simon and Schuster, 1988), 203.

2. Edward R. Harrison, *Masks of the Universe* (New York: Macmillan, 1985), 252.

3. Fred Hoyle, "The Universe: Past and Present Reflections," *Annual Review of Astronomy and Astrophysics* 20 (1982).

Chapter 48: Why should life on earth be viewed as evidence for the supernatural when so many other planets can sustain life?

1. Peter D. Ward and Donald Brownlee, *Rare Earth* (New York: Copernicus, 2000), 220. For an excellent discussion of the importance of plate tectonics, see pages 191–220.

2. Hugh Ross, "Probability for Life on Earth," *Reasons to Believe*, April 1, 2004, www.reasons. org/articles/probability-for-life-on-earth. Also see Hugh Ross, *Improbable Planet* (Grand Rapids, MI: Baker, 2016).

Chapter 49: What if there is an infinite number of universes, and we're just fortunate to be in one that sustains life?
1. Clifford Longley, "Focusing on Theism," *London Times*, January 21, 1989.
2. Lee Strobel, *The Case for Faith* (Grand Rapids, MI: Zondervan, 2000), 78–79.
3. John Polkinghorne, *Science and Theology* (Minneapolis: Fortress Press, 1998), 38.
4. Richard Swinburne, *Is There a God?* (Oxford, UK: Oxford University Press, 1995), 68.

Chapter 51: What was the evidence that convinced you Jesus really rose from the dead?
1. These points about Jesus' resurrection have been strongly influenced by my friend Gary Habermas and his book *The Historical Jesus* (Joplin, MO: College Press, 1996).

2. Lee Strobel, *The Case for Christ* (Grand Rapids, MI: Zondervan, 1998), 90–91.

3. Habermas, *The Historical Jesus*, 251.

Chapter 52: Much of the evidence for the resurrection is based on eyewitnesses. But aren't they often unreliable?

1. See 1 Corinthians 15:3ff.

Chapter 53: What about the discrepancies between the Gospels? Do they discredit the miracle of the resurrection?

1. Simon Greenleaf, *The Testimony of the Evangelists* (Grand Rapids, MI: Baker, 1984), vii.

Chapter 54: What kind of impact does the miracle of Jesus' resurrection have on individual lives?

1. Kerry and Chris Shook, *Find Your Miracle: How the Miracles of Jesus Can Change Your Life Today* (New York: Waterbrook, 2016), 204.

2. See Lee Strobel, *The Case for Christ*, 186–203.

3. See Stan Telchin, *Betrayed!* (Grand Rapids, MI: Chosen, 1982).

Chapter 57: How can I handle the disappointment of *not* having my prayers answered . . . of not getting a miracle?

    1. See Matthew 27:46 and Psalm 22:1.

Chapter 58: When miracles don't happen and suffering continues, which worldview offers the best answers?

    1. See John 11:1–44.

Chapter 60: You've convinced me miracles really do happen. But what difference should that make in my life?

    1. Richard L. Purtill, "Defining Miracles" in Douglas Geivett and Gary R. Habermas, eds., *In Defense of Miracles* (Downers Grove, IL: InterVarsity, 1997), 72.

    2. Kerry and Chris Shook, *Find Your Miracle: How the Miracles of Jesus Can Change Your Life Today* (New York: Waterbrook, 2016), 204.

    3. Shook, *Find Your Miracle*, 191.